No Longer Strangers
The Practice of Radical Hospitality

"… explodes the myths that allow immigration to be used as a wedge issue in our communities."
— Edith Rasell, PhD
Minister for Economic Justice, Justice and Witness Ministries
United Church of Christ

"No Longer Strangers invites us to set aside fear-invoking terms such as "illegal aliens" and to offer hospitality to the "men and women alone" who work in fields and kitchens and back rooms all over this country, often invisibly, but bearing the gifts of God."
— Dick Matgen, former Senior Program Officer
Peninsula Community Foundation

"Full of intelligence, humanity and understanding, *No Longer Strangers* shows how faith, when practiced in the context of today's complex world, still has the power to transform lives."
— Tessa Rouverol Callejo
FAITHS Program and Civic Engagement Officer
The San Francisco Foundation

"I have never lived in a rural farming community, nor in a community that depended on workers who—for many reasons—are invisible. But now I feel I've lived that experience—thanks to the authenticity of this book. I loved the details, I wanted to take it all in, down to the very last crumb."
— Migs Carter, Multicultural Youth Advocate

"No Longer Strangers tells the story of the development of an organization that recognizes, values, supports and includes migrant workers. If you really want to make a difference in your community, this is how you do it."
— Beryl Rullman, M. Ed., Coaching Nonprofit Executives

"No matter what happens in the world around us, radical hospitality can soften the harsh word and lighten the load. For those migrant workers caught up in a life of toil, Puente has eased the burden of unfair immigration policies and made the South Coast feel a little more like home. This is the story of how Puente began."
— Kerry Lobel
Executive Director, Puente

"Some of us thought the hard part would be getting here. But, when we got here, we had other problems, and it wasn't that simple...It is really hard to find myself so far away from the land where I was born. But when we encounter this support from you, we can show our families that we are being taken care of. It makes them so happy. They thank God, and they pray for all of you, too."
— A worker from Oaxaca, one of The Men Alone,
from the video at www.no-longer-strangers.org

No Longer Strangers

The Practice of Radical Hospitality

❧❧

Rev. Wendy J. Taylor
with
Margaret Kimball Cross

Gloria Anzaldúa quote used with permission of the Gloria E. Anzaldúa Literary Trust. All rights reserved.

Joan Chittister quote from *The Rule of Benedict, A Spirituality for the 21st Century*. Quoted with permission of The Crossroads Publishing Company. All rights reserved.

The Rev. Martin Copenhaver quote from the United Church of Christ's Stillspeaking Daily Devotional website. Used with permission of the author. All rights reserved.

Puente service area map created by Peter R. Cross. All rights reserved.

Clarissa Pinkola Estés quote excerpted from "Letter To A Young Activist During Troubled Times: Do Not Lose Heart, We Were Made For These Times" ©1990, 2011. Quoted with kind permission of author and publisher. All rights reserved. Permissions: ngandelman@gmail.com

Etty Hilleseum quote from *An Interrupted Life: The Journal of a Young Jewish Woman, 1941-1943*. Used with permission of Persephone Books. All rights reserved.

Thich Nhat Hanh quote from *Being Peace.* Copyright 1987. Used with permission of Parallax Press, Berkeley, CA. www.parallax.org.

All biblical quotations are from the
***New Revised Standard Version* Bible unless otherwise noted.**

New Revised Standard Version Bible. Copyright 1989 by The Division of Christian Education of the National Council of the Churches of Christ in the U.S.A. Used with permission. All rights reserved.

The Message Bible. Copyright 2002. Used with permission of NavPress Publishing Group. All rights reserved

Every attempt has been made to get all permissions, copyrights, and authorizations. We apologize for any omissions in this respect and will be pleased to make appropriate recognition in any future edition.

The authors are donating a portion of the net proceeds from this book to Puente and other immigrant justice organizations.

ISBN-13: 978-1-46099-159-6
ISBN-10: 1-460-99159-1
Library of Congress: 2011911204

To the Rev. Dan Aprá,
my mentor and *mi abuelo en mi corazón*,
grandfather in my heart,
and
to Ray Nelson,
my co-worker, dear friend and
hermano del espíritu, brother in spirit.

These two dear men were the strongholds for my vision
and ministry. They died within months of each other
in the spring of 2010, before we could publish this book.

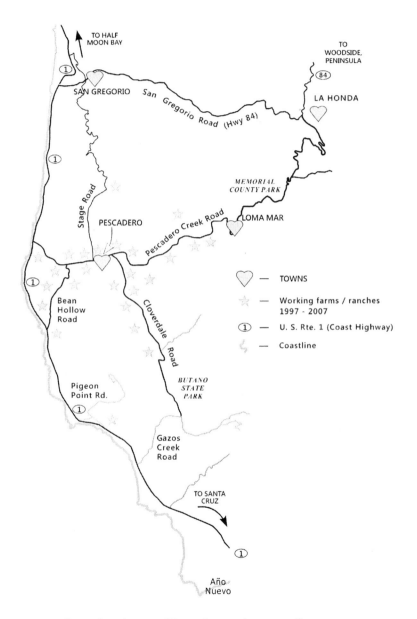

TO HALF
MOON BAY

TO
WOODSIDE,
PENINSULA

①

84

SAN GREGORIO

LA HONDA

San Gregorio Road (Hwy 84)

①

Stage Road

MEMORIAL
COUNTY PARK

PESCADERO

Pescadero Creek Road

LOMA MAR

— TOWNS

①

Cloverdale Road

— Working farms / ranches
1997 - 2007

Bean
Hollow
Road

① — U. S. Rte. 1 (Coast Highway)

— Coastline

BUTANO
STATE
PARK

Pigeon
Point Rd.

①

Gazos
Creek
Road

TO SANTA
CRUZ

①

Año
Nuevo

See color photos of Pescadero and surrounding areas
in the gallery section of www.no-longer-strangers.org/

CONTENTS

Foreword

Twenty years ago, Janet Murphy and I each came independently to the South San Mateo Coast. Separately, we decided to look around for ways to contribute to the community, and because we both spoke Spanish as a second language, we were led into relationships with the Spanish-speaking community that are still active to this day.

When we arrived, migrant education in the La Honda-Pescadero School District was a tumultuous issue. Early on, I became acquainted with parents who were very unhappy with the way their children were being treated, and after reading a newspaper article about the neglect of Spanish-speaking students in the schools, I decided to volunteer to work with these students. That job led, in turn, to a class where I taught English as a Second Language (ESL) to Spanish-speaking adults, a class that took place in housing owned by a nursery.

I had some training in ESL teaching, but it was mostly "sink or swim" for me, just as it was for the children who had been thrown into a school situation where they had to learn in a new language—or be treated as failures. I was never offered materials or advice. Except for a little help from Project Read I was on my own.

Because of my relationship with students and families, I met some remarkable people who were working hard to improve services to the English-learner school population. But I also became aware of the gulf between the Mexican part of the population and most of the residents, including school board members and administration. I learned of injustices (sometimes worse than those I had read about in mailings from the United Farm Workers) suffered by my students and their friends at work. And I had almost no idea of where to get help.

After a year of tutoring at the school and about three years of teaching adult classes, I found out about the ESL classes offered at the Pescadero Community Church. I decided to go to a Sunday service to find out more about them. It was here that I ultimately joined forces with Janet Murphy, who was in her second year running an ESL program that had been started by others in 1988. I was happy to have the support of both Janet and the church in this work—especially the financial and moral support of the Ladies' Guild. It was wonderful to find people of good will in our community who wanted to reach out to all who needed their help and kindness.

Our staff—Janet, myself, and Ray Nelson—were often augmented by assistants and temporary teachers. Church members went out of their way to thank us personally and in public during church services and meetings. And others in our coastside community also offered encouragement. All this was most welcome especially during those times when I became overwhelmed by the loneliness and hardships of my students and needed motivation to keep going.

Janet got to know several workers by hiring them to spend some of their "free" hours working in her very ambitious garden. These contacts led her into friendships with the men and a few women who were here alone, and also with various families. Because she spoke Spanish and because she exuded compassion, these folks presented her with a constant stream of needs from documents that needed translation to trips for medical help. Janet became very interested in the family and village connections of these Mexican fellow residents. By the time Wendy Taylor arrived in Pescadero, Janet was probably the best-known American among local Mexicans, as well as one of the few Americans familiar with where the workers lived in and around Pescadero.

During her time as a teacher at Pescadero High School, Wendy asked Janet and me to help her become better acquainted with the community. Janet took her on a tour of the ranches and explained the shifting seasons of employment and the way the workers tended to follow other members from their family and village to Pescadero. Since I was then teaching at a ranch (perhaps the most humane place for living and working in the area), I introduced Wendy to families there.

By the time Wendy began her ministry, some efforts to coordinate community services had already taken place, starting—to my knowledge—with initiatives by Judy McKee and Carol Young Holt; and local people, the school district, and outside agencies were starting to cooperate. However, Janet and I were not aware of any outreach efforts to the single men on the ranches, nor do we remember anyone trying to help with their safety, pay, or housing issues.

We were pleased when Wendy proposed to work with the Mexicans—and even happier that after becoming familiar with the community and its existing programs, she chose to focus on The Men Alone. Along with others in the congregation, we supported the connection of the church with Wendy's plans and program.

The work described in this book changed the tenor of life in Pescadero—dramatically for Mexican workers, and substantially for other residents. With regard to working conditions, and even the fight for basic justice for workers, Puente Ministry was the pre-eminent, and often the *single,* source of help.

In my work now, I have—through Puente—resources and contacts that make my teaching a pleasure, and that provide help when my students come to me with problems—from minor to tragic. Janet is still helping her long-time Mexican friends, and their friends—and teaching at the *La Sala* gatherings described in this book. And we are happy to know that we are backed by an amazing entity—Puente Ministry—that was once just Reverend Wendy's dream.

— Barbara Turner
Veteran ESL Teacher in La Honda and Pescadero

Introduction

Only the Creator is perfect.

— Theresa Wescott, Menominee Elder

This is a work of non-fiction, but it was written from our memories of events, not from notes or recorded materials; hence, it may vary from your memories, if you were there. Our story has a beginning and, for us, an ending, but the larger story goes on, and you can read about Puente's current activities at *www.mypuente.org*. Events are not necessarily in chronological order, but rather grouped more by area of emphasis. Names and some details are altered honoring the privacy of those involved. Not everyone is included by name. Our hope is to give the reader a sense of what it was like to be there with us through it all.

We decided to tell our story through Wendy's voice, and, naturally, in English, but we have included *Spanish in italics* to remind the reader that this was truly a bi-lingual experience. Conversations characteristically drifted in and out of both languages, and our experiences were always a mix. ¡*Qué sabroso* (how delicious)! Although it may seem abrupt, we are not putting English first because we want to give monolingual English speakers the opportunity to be sensitive to both languages. We cannot assume that we all understand each other, or that the English language has an exclusive on the spirit of the message.

Many times we have used words that look alike in Spanish and English but that have slightly different meanings. For example, the word *café* means a restaurant in English, and a hot beverage—coffee—in Spanish. The easiest Spanish words for English speakers to understand are the cognates: *no* (no); and those with nearly the same spelling: *estereo* (stereo), *chocolate*

(chocolate), or *carro* (car). To pronounce these words in Spanish would confound many of us unfamiliar with the vowel and consonant sounds in Spanish. For example, *chocolate* sounds like *choe-koe-law-tay*.

Moreover, words can sometimes be "false" cognates. Wendy tells a story of how such words confounded her early in her teaching career. During her first day in Puerto Rico teaching in the Volunteers in Service to America (VISTA) Corps, she apologized to her students for her academic Spanish, which was not Puerto Rican in vocabulary, intonation, or pronunciation. "*Estoy tan embarazada!* (I am so embarrassed!)" she said. Or so she thought she said. But *embarazada* does not mean "embarrassed." It means "pregnant." And very definitely, Wendy was not announcing her pregnancy!

The word *taller*, another false cognate, looks like the English word denoting height. In fact, in Spanish, it is pronounced "*tie-yair*," and it means "workshop," "lab," "studio" or "factory." *Caro* means "expensive" in Spanish—not "car" as we might mistakenly assume. I hope the reader will reach for and find the true meaning of each conversation that mixes Spanish and English in this book.

Language is, after all, one of the primary ways we all share our thoughts, needs, feelings, and ideas. One goal of this book is to guide the reader into a deeper appreciation of that bilingual and bicultural experience.

— Margaret Kimball Cross

Preface

You shall have one law
For the stranger
And for the citizen:
For I am the Lord your God.

— Leviticus 24:22, adapted from NRSV

It seems clear to me that God doesn't differentiate between "citizens" and "strangers." Therefore, neither will I. This story, my own life story, is about how one woman was called to bridge-building, reconciling, and making friends, especially with those whom others called strangers.

My heart's desire, which became my life mission, was born out of the hope and love my family and God created in me when I was very young. My dad instilled in me the idea that I could do anything, and my mother taught me to share kindness and acceptance with any who did not know, or who had never experienced, kindness.

In this story, my co-author and I share with you the ways through which, by holy covenant between our God and ourselves, we can all widen our community, as we *"seek justice, love kindness and walk humbly with our God."* (Micah 6:8)

From my wife, Ellen, I learned the term *cultural humility.* It means being *teachable*, being ready to learn the value of another's culture, and being willing and able to respect that culture. I feel cultural humility as both a teacher and a student; and I believe that cultural humility and universal love need to be standard practices among us all. But too often, when faced with a person or culture that is not our own, we lack the vision to see our common humanity. Instead, we may fear for our personal safety or we may feel anger at the potential threat to our financial security posed by the "other."

At the heart of my faith is the belief that we must no longer be strangers. When we accept the divine grace of respectfulness and take the time to truly encounter one another, we always find that we have much in common, that we are truly "One." In both the book of Matthew—"*I was a stranger and you welcomed me*"—and the writings of the Apostle Paul to the Ephesians—"*So then, you are no longer strangers . . .(but) members of the household of God*"—this fundamental belief is affirmed. *All* are to be accorded radical hospitality.

Throughout history, the practice of radical hospitality has carried the image of extravagant, whole-hearted, over-the-top welcome. St. Benedict included it in his spiritual principles centuries ago, and it surfaces today in my own spiritual practice. We must remember that English-speaking people have no corner on this practice. It is inherent in many of the world's cultures.

Spanish-speaking cultures, especially, offer genuine welcome. In the Spanish tradition, b*ienvenido* (welcome) is embodied in the common aphorism *mi casa es su casa* (my home is your home). It captures the willingness to, and the joy of, taking into our hearts and homes *neighbors, strangers* or *beloveds*—anyone in God's holy creation. I took it on faith that Pescadero, our tiny village, would embody this practice in both its English- and Spanish-speaking communities. And it did.

It is our common *response-ability* to meet every member of our community with universal love, stewardship, and faithfulness. We are one people, one planet, one family in the Divine's whole and holy creation. The depth of our rootedness in God's words though clear to us often we stray and find ourselves isolating, judging, and harming others, or feeling our entitlement. We are the only ones who can change our beliefs and practices, and we must do so by embracing that which allows us to bring abundance to all. When we do this, we also engage in a healing process for ourselves.

In the practice of radical hospitality, there is no place for actions that isolate another, for judging or harming anyone. We must set aside any feelings of entitlement or privilege on the basis of race, economic class, or education. We certainly need to avoid patronizing—or assuming that we are the ones *who have to do everything for them*, as if *we know the only path for them*. Our humility reminds us that we are *not the only* culture, nor are we the *right* culture. We *do not* have the only answers. We can learn God's ways and make them ours.

Even in these difficult times, I am reminded, *"If God is for us, who can be against us?"* (Romans 8:31). My lifelong sustenance is the hope that nothing in my life will take God away from me. This verse continues, echoing in my heart:

> Who (indeed) shall separate us from the love of Christ? Shall tribulation, or distress, or persecution, or famine, or nakedness, or peril, or sword? … For I am persuaded that neither death nor life, nor angels nor principalities nor (rulers), nor things present nor things to come, nor height nor depth, nor any other created thing shall be able to separate us from the love of God… .
>
> — Romans 8:35, 38-39

With this assurance, Puente, our bridge, was built on the *roots* (Latin: *radix*) of compassion; and thus, it was *radical* hospitality we offered. The term *radical* has been co-opted to mean "way out there" or "too far politically in one direction or the other." However, it is the tap root of our faith, fed by love, hope, justice, courage, compassion, and trusting care for all equally in Creation.

We all may choose to be fed by the divine succor of shared respectfulness as we take the time to encounter one another; and if we do so, we will soon come to know that there *is* only the *common good*. Then, as nurtured human beings, we may respond through hospitality (Latin: *hospitalitas*), which means receiving someone as a guest or being a host. Even the Old English term *wilcuma* includes in its meaning the idea that people share a cordial greeting, are gladly accepting of, and offer a warm welcome to the recently arrived visitor.

I have been blessed with many experiences that have taught me how to change, and how to blend and commune with people outside my comfort zone. Thanks be to God! And I will continue in that spirit. My past, including my facility with Spanish, brought me a unique call to a community where Spanish was spoken. And it turned out that this call included building a bridge ministry of welcome, reconciliation, and radical hospitality. That I found such work was miraculous!

Today we live in a critical time for all the migrant laborers and families. They are economic refugees who live among us, unable to come and go across our borders as they once did. How could I not live by the Scripture of my childhood? How could I ignore this call as an adult?

There is one more verse that has echoed in my head ever since my pastoral internship, and it is this: *"I chose you, you did not choose me."* (John 15:11).

Each of these verses has spoken deeply to me. I grew up holding tightly to them and pondering how I would be directed to live them out. They are as important to me now as they were when I first encountered them in my childhood, at seminary, during my student clergy years, and at ordination. They are also the root of ministry for Ellen, my life-long partner for twenty-seven years. Her mission, as a former Sister of St. Joseph of Carondelet, has always been "to unite neighbor with neighbor, and neighbor with God." It is extraordinary and mysterious how we each shared that sense of call prior to meeting, and how we both still deeply love to uphold each other as spouses in our calls to minister.

This story was written *to honor* all those men and women who have worked and lived in Pescadero, California, both in the past decade and long before Puente Ministry was born. It was also written *to encourage* other people of faith who are longing to act out of their compassion to alleviate the difficulties facing the "strangers" in their communities. And this story is a call *to celebrate* the very real joy that comes from practicing radical and extravagant hospitality! Faith without borders, indeed! *¡Solo Dios basta* (God alone is enough)! Hospitality becomes a precious new way to worship.

Through this story, I hope that we have served up *el sabor* (the flavor) of the Puente (Bridge) Ministry for our readers. It was, indeed, a daunting task. But as God is my witness, we have walked the walk and given our all. In gratitude we offer it to God's glory. And we hope that you, too, may know that *¡sí, se puede* (yes, you can)!

My personal practice of meditating over the years with the Benedictine Sisters of the Guadalupe Retreat Center in Cuernavaca, Morelos, Mexico, has filled my soul with inspiration. It is based on the writings of Sister Joan Chittister, Order of Saint Benedict, who reminds us:

> For the Benedictine heart
> The reception of the poor
> Is an essential part of
> Going toward God.
>
> —The Rule of Benedict:
> A Spirituality for the 21st Century, p. 231

— Rev. Wendy J. Taylor

So then, you are no longer
strangers and aliens,
but you are citizens with the saints
and also members of
the household of God...
— Ephesians 2:19

1

The Call

We lean like plants lean toward a window,
even though they may never have seen the sun.
We lean, with longing hearts,
toward God's vision of the kingdom to come.

— Rev. Martin Copenhaver
Daily Seeds, in God is Still Speaking

It's funny how life's path meanders. Only looking back can I see where I was headed all along. Now, pausing, I can see clearly that I was headed for this *puente* (bridge) all my life.

On that day in 1997 when Ellen and I tossed our overnight bags in the truck and headed for the Coast, I had nothing more on my mind than checking in at the hotel and relaxing on the beach. At last we would have a respite from our work to sleep, eat, talk and re-create! A few weeks earlier we had attended an AIDS benefit at the Kohl Mansion in Burlingame. Ellen's work community was there, supporting the big fundraiser, and during the auction we had won the bid on an overnight stay at the San Benito Inn in Half Moon Bay, California. What an unexpected gift! I never imagined that such a chance encounter would radically change our lives for the next decade.

I was fully and joyously engaged at that time in my ministry at the Congregational Church of Belmont, United

Church of Christ, and Ellen was loving her position (and working much too hard) as Prevention Services Coordinator for the San Mateo County Health Department's AIDS Program. That day we both just needed to get away. As we soared west on Highway 92, past Crystal Springs reservoir, then up and over Skyline ridge, and down into Half Moon Bay, we could feel the concerns of the week flowing out of our minds, leaving us free. As we watched rows of stock in burgundy, yellow, cream, white and purple stream by, we both inhaled deeply the sweet fragrances of those flowers wafting through our open windows.

It is amazing how, in the space of six or seven short miles, often only ten minutes or so, you can go from many urban places in the Bay Area to rural settings. That day we went from the urban bayside towns of Belmont and San Mateo to the very rural coastside. From multistory buildings, acres of homes, and hundreds of cars making their way up and down freeways, we entered a place of nearly deserted beaches, a patchwork of farm fields, and tourist shops bordering a variety of old cottages nestled against new housing developments. It is an entirely different world.

Half Moon Bay was already a special, sacred space for me as I had been driving over the hill to Miramar Beach for my Monday "Sabbath" reflection every week for some time. Here, with the surf as my background music, I would sit for hours absorbing the quiet, meditating, eating my picnic lunch, and reading my favorite books. I simply allowed God's presence to fill my inner being.

These coastside beaches were often wrapped in fog, and the only people I would see were dog walkers and surf fishermen. They are not beaches for paddling in the surf as the water is quite chilly and the waves often dangerous. The unwary walker venturing too close to an incoming rogue wave has been known to be swept out to sea and lost! For me, it was always enough just to listen to the regular ebb and flow of the waves, absorbing their rhythm like a mantra. This time I planned to enjoy all this and more with my partner.

Strolling through the lobby of the hotel, I picked up a copy of the local weekly newspaper and noticed a headline about Silicon Valley monies being designated for local literacy programs, a "lighthouse literacy focus for the next three years." This program was to take place at the La Honda-Pescadero Unified School District just eighteen miles south on the Coast Highway—a district that was quite small, 70 percent Spanish-speaking, and very short of resources. As a former teacher, I was intrigued: it sounded like someone was reaching out to the underserved, and the schools might welcome an extra boost.

I remembered Pescadero vaguely from a study I had done about ten years earlier, right after I finished seminary. My mentor, the Rev. Dan Aprá, had commissioned me to complete a demographic survey of the Bay Area, identifying places where there were concentrations of Spanish-speaking people. His dream was to establish a special ministry and grow a new church with this immigrant community on behalf of the Northern California and Nevada Conference of the United Church of Christ. Nothing like this had ever existed in our conference.

I saw that the centerpiece of the school program was a plan to improve literacy in English. It centered on a curriculum tool, which each teacher would be asked to follow consistently. The steps included age-appropriate writing, spelling, classroom reading, and leisure-time reading activities. Students would read and evaluate each other's work; parents would be given the same curriculum tools to help their children do homework; and all classes, at every level, would use the same approaches and guides. I thought about how California schools had been struggling for years, trying various strategies with mixed success to unify mono-lingual and multi-cultural students under a single language. In the face of coming changes in the law, schools would be trying yet again, and I wondered whether this program would offer real progress.

Reading on, I learned that the state legislature planned simultaneously to eliminate the popular bilingual classes in most schools. According to the plan, these classes could continue only if twenty concerned parents got together and petitioned for special consideration. This would be hard to do in most Spanish-speaking neighborhoods. I could imagine that it would be nearly impossible in rural Pescadero. I remembered from my teaching experiences in a rural school in Erie, Colorado, that the average class size was likely too small to have twenty parents represented. These intimate classes were both the bane and blessing of "country schools."

That noon we drove south to Pescadero to eat lunch at Duarte's Tavern. Duarte's started in 1894 when the current owner's great-grandfather Frank brought a barrel of whiskey from Santa Cruz and placed it on the very bar in use today. The price then was ten cents for one whiskey, two bits for three.[1] Since that day in 1894, it has served as a landmark for those traveling the Pacific Coast Highway. Food was added to the menu some years later, and today Duarte's reputation for fine food has eclipsed its early role as a tavern.

As we drove south, rounding the headland and looking down into the surf, we spotted baby otters swimming with their moms among the rocks and tide pools. Those little otters, with their whiskered faces, were splashing, diving, and skimming along the water on their backs. They, of course, were oblivious to our stares; but, we *had* to stop, we could not take our eyes off of them. It was a special moment we were privileged to share.

As we returned to the highway and came to the top of the hill overlooking the Pescadero marsh, I spotted three coyotes patrolling the nearby ridge. We made time to slow down, turn around, and watch those sentinels high on the hill. From the sky came a peregrine falcon, who landed gracefully on one of many power poles surrounding that marsh. I had heard my bird-watching friends rave about the opportunities to observe the various migrations that regularly stopped here—and now I had confirmation that it was so.

Earlier we had driven through a rain shower, and as we turned off the highway onto the road leading into town, a

---

[1] http://www.duartestavern.com/history.html

double rainbow arched in the eastern sky. It seemed to rest on the hills, surrounding and protecting the village, and—I thought—welcoming us. Having left behind the familiar city sights and sounds, we felt embraced by these miraculous and glorious reminders of our Creator.

Our souls were full! Now we prepared to fill our bodies. At Duarte's, dining is cozy and very informal. Its highly polished, heavy wooden tables are placed close together and greetings often fly from person to person. As we sat down, I noticed a woman sitting at a table across from us with a baby sleeping in a detachable car seat. I don't know why I spoke to her, but I did. I asked how old her baby was.

"Ten months," she responded, and went on to explain that she was on her lunch break. I was immediately impressed. Here was someone who could take her baby to her job: she must work in a good place!

She told me that she worked in the library at Pescadero High School, not far away, just up the street. We continued chatting after our orders were taken. I told her that while I was currently a pastor, I had been a high school English and Spanish teacher. I also mentioned that I was bilingual and had experience working in Spanish-speaking countries. After reflecting for a moment, I added that I sometimes thought of returning to teaching, perhaps when I retired. Her face lit up and she launched into an enthusiastic pitch about how badly her school needed bilingual teachers.

"You're bilingual! And you're an experienced teacher! Why don't you apply?" she nudged. I heard a tiny voice, somewhere deep inside, whispering, *Hmm, this is a familiar tug. I just might do it!*

That day the crabmelt, spinach salad, and olallieberry pie were especially *sabroso* (tasty). Duarte's owners grow many of the fresh green vegetables and berries used in the restaurant in a small, luscious garden patch behind their building. The international menu features both an *alcachofa* (artichoke) soup and a *chile* (chili) soup. The locals are quick to suggest that you order it *mixto* (mixed) for an exquisite taste combo. The chef swirls the two together artistically creating a delightful yin/yang design almost too gorgeous to eat. It was definitely well worth the drive down the coast.

Duarte's always offers a long list of the fresh fruit pies: *fresa* (strawberry), *ruibarbo* (rhubarb), *albaricoque* (apricot), *melocotón* (peach) and *moras mixtas* (mixed berries). That day the pie was so wonderful, in fact, that we came back a few weeks later to show off Duarte's to Ellen's mom, Marcella, and her friend, Cathy, both of whom were visiting from St. Louis. When we took our seats, we found ourselves once again right across from the woman with her baby!

There are no accidents.

I remember greeting her almost as though we were old friends. Immediately, she poured out the story of how she had nearly lost this precious baby to a mysterious illness just the night before. The doctor she had called in San Francisco, knowing her to be an experienced mom, took her panic seriously. He said he would meet her at the hospital as soon as she could get there. The family went directly to the hospital in San Francisco, fifty miles north on Pacific Coast Highway 1, and the illness was treated successfully—as I witnessed by the rosy-cheeked little one cuddled up on her lap.

She seemed remarkably candid to me, a stranger. When she had finished her story, she assured me that she had received support from her church through the crisis. Clearly she was not confiding in me in order to seek pastoral care. She had quite a different purpose! She turned back to me and asked if I'd applied yet for the teaching position. Such a persistent woman! Perhaps hers was the voice of Yahweh incarnate.

That was the last straw, all the "call" I needed. The possibility of returning to teaching in a setting like this had been running through my thoughts, hanging around in the back of my mind, since our first encounter. When we finished eating, I walked over to the school district office, and picked up that application. I must have looked a bit odd: I was decked out in my Oakland Athletics regalia—socks, shorts, shirt and cap—in anticipation of the evening baseball game. *¡Fíjese* (imagine my nerve)!

I completed the paperwork, and within a week was invited to interview with Bonnie, the district superintendent. On the same day I interviewed with Bonnie, I also met the high school principal, Don. We talked for hours and toured the small school building; and at the end of the interview, Don offered me the position. I told him I would think it over.

I prayed over this process. How could I leave my current church—the Congregational Church of Belmont? I had been co-pastor there with the Rev. John Brooke for nearly five years, and I was well into a second five years of service as solo pastor. Moreover, my call to serve had come after several discouraging rejections from other congregations because of my sexual orientation. Ellen and I had been warmly welcomed at the Belmont church; and the congregation had embraced an Open and Affirming position[2] that allowed us to welcome other new people—men, women and families—some of whom were living with HIV/AIDS. I had baptized, married and buried dozens who would not have found such a loving reception in their home congregations. This faithful and just church had truly made me feel that I, too, was a member of the family. How could I leave all that?

As it happened, that very weekend Ellen and I were scheduled to attend the annual meeting of our church conference at Asilomar, a beautiful conference grounds near Monterey. We would be the voting representatives for the Belmont church. It was our family tradition to stay a couple of days afterwards for a mini-vacation at nearby Pismo Beach. On this occasion we knew we needed time for discernment about this potential new "call" from Pescadero. Before we left the Bay

---

[2] A church policy that welcomes all into full membership, leadership, and the ordained ministry—especially gay, lesbian, bisexual, transgender, queer, questioning and intersex individuals; those of diverse racial, class, ethnic, cultural backgrounds; and those with mobility limitations.

Area, I asked the principal from Pescadero High to call me at Pismo Beach for my response to his offer.

At the conference meeting, I spent a good amount of time talking face to face with the moderator of the Belmont church about this new opportunity in Pescadero. If I were to take the job, he and I would need to carefully plan my exit strategy to ensure that the congregation was cared for during the transition. It was a poignant time for me—so poignant that people around me began to wonder if I had lost a family member. Some said I looked like I was in the midst of grieving. In fact I was deeply saddened by the prospect that I might very well be leaving the Belmont church. *¡Primero Dios* (we leave it in God's hands)!

At Pismo, Ellen and I mulled, prayed, talked, and cried. Both of us knew full well about powerful "calls" to ministry. We had each received calls in the past, not knowing where they would lead us, and we had each entered into new communities willing to hear what was needed. Indeed, this mutual awareness of "receiving a call" had been the foundation of our relationship during the first months after we met at seminary in 1984.

As we talked that day, Ellen recalled her own experiences as a Sister of St. Joseph of Carondelet. During a decade of service in Wisconsin, she had worked as a pastoral associate on the Menominee Indian Reservation. And in Lowndes County, Alabama, she and another sister had renovated an old train station to house a new after-school program. In both situations, she had felt and responded to those unexpected nudges to action.

I had built up a background of varied experiences while living and working with people in Puerto Rico, Central and South America, and Mexico, and in all those places, I had been received graciously into the various cultures. It became clear that my Spanish/English language experience was finally to become the foundation of a visionary ministry for me. Perhaps all those other assignments had been designed to prepare me "for such a time as this."[3]

When the principal did call, I said yes! Ellen and I both knew from all our past years of ministering that God would be our nurturer and sustainer, and we confidently prepared to take up this new call.

When we returned to Belmont, I rushed to call my friend Margaret. While there were many people I'd grown to care about in the Belmont church, Margaret was the one I wanted to tell myself. I trusted our friendship enough to be confident that once she put all the pieces together, she would know why I had to go. When it came to the working of the Holy Spirit, she always "got it." However, I wanted to be sure she heard the news from me first—and face to face. I wanted her to understand and support my decision. And so I invited her for coffee.

A few years earlier, Margaret had come to me for pastoral counsel. After she had made a commitment to recovery, she continued with the counseling. It was a difficult time for her, and during the months that followed we met often. I got to know her very well. We shared our faith journeys, the stories of our struggles and triumphs, and the conviction that our deepest desire is to listen for that voice of God in the ordinary activities of life. Over the years that followed, Margaret took an active role as a lay leader in the church, serving on the board of trustees and later as moderator. We had worked through many potential difficulties within the church over the years, and we found that our perspectives and methods of problem solving complemented each other. Now, I looked forward to sharing my decision with her.

"You are going to do . . . what?" she stammered. Her initial disbelief was profound. Then she thought about it for a moment, looked me square in the face, and said, "Yes, I can see exactly why you must."

By the third week of June, 1997, I had said goodbye to those dear parishioners in Belmont, and I was teaching summer

---

[3] Esther 4:14

school and sharing my Spanish gifts with the middle school youth of Pescadero. Earlier that same month, Ellen and I had sold our San Mateo condominium, which was co-owned with the Belmont church. Miraculously, on one of my "Sabbath Mondays" in Half Moon Bay, I discovered the only available modular home for sale at Princeton Harbor, at the north end of Half Moon Bay, and we quickly bought it. This mini-village development is just over the cliffs from the famous Maverick's surfing beach. We were quite suddenly transformed into "Coastsiders."

I had heard of the only Protestant church in Pescadero because it happened to be affiliated with United Church of Christ, and I knew that it was staffed by a group of retired pastors. When I called and talked with the lead pastor, he welcomed me to join in their preaching rotation. Suddenly I had the best of both worlds! I was a "bi-vocational" pastor. During the week, I would work as a high school teacher and I would make pastoral calls, and on some Sundays I would lead worship. This situation reminded me of what Belmont's seminary intern, now the Reverend Karen Gale, had observed about parish ministries. She believed that "a bi-vocational context is the only true context out of which to minister." Now, I would be doing just that. Clearly we need to learn from our students!

Monday through Friday I would teach English as a Second Language and English to high school youth who spoke mostly Spanish as their first language. Many of them spoke *only* Spanish in their homes. And on Sundays, I would worship and pray with men, women, and children who spoke *only* English.

Before Ellen and I packed up to move to our new coastside home, Margaret and I made a commitment to meet for coffee each week. Now that I was no longer her pastor, I was free to accept her invitation to be her "sponsor." I could coach her as she worked the steps of her program. And I knew that her perspectives as my sounding board would be helpful as I threaded my way through all the new situations I would surely be meeting.

Our plan was that she would drive over the hill and I would drive up the coast to meet at a coffee shop in Half Moon Bay each week. There for an hour or so we would share our life experiences. I could hardly wait to tell her about the village of Pescadero that I saw beyond Duarte's!

When we next met, I described to her the nearly one hundred houses, several businesses, and three schools I had seen so far in Pescadero. People were telling me that the town was home to about six hundred inhabitants, with maybe as many as six thousand more folks in the surrounding un-incorporated area, including the villages of La Honda, Loma Mar, and San Gregorio. Many of the families with school-age children spoke only Spanish, while most of the long-time residents—middle-aged and older—spoke only English, though they might have Portuguese, Italian, Japanese, or Chinese heritage.

After pouring out my description of the town, Margaret pondered and then remarked, "Clearly there must be some big gaps within this little community."

I thought to myself, *Well, maybe that's why I'm here.*

2

My Response

Is it not to share your bread with the hungry,
and bring the homeless poor into your house;
when you see the naked, to cover them,
and not to hide yourself from your own kin?
Then your light shall break forth like the dawn,
and your healing shall spring up quickly...
Then you shall call, and the Lord will answer;
you shall cry for help, and the Lord will say,
Here I am.

— Isaiah 58:7-8a, 9

Strangers, yes. When Ellen and I parked and stepped up the front steps of the Pescadero Community Church, we were total strangers to everyone there. Although we had eaten at Duarte's for years, and although I had been hired at the school district, neither of us knew a soul at the church. Yet we stepped boldly through the big redwood doors, picked up a worship bulletin to share, and walked down the aisle.

The church, built in 1867, just two years after the end of the Civil War, reflected the style of sanctuary construction popular in that era. Aisles down each side created a section of pews on outer sides of the room, and a wider section of seating in the center, with a dividing barrier down the middle. I was told that this style of seating was created to force women and men to sit on opposite sides of the sanctuary. Hard to imagine a seating arrangement like that today with families spilling in, friends greeting each other, and kids bouncing here and there.

As quickly and smoothly as we slid into the pew and flipped open a hymnal, we passed from being "strangers" to being "congregants." I knew that this little church had adopted an Open and Affirming statement and that we would be officially welcomed. But even as we returned the smiles and answered the conventional questions, we both knew that there were likely some in this congregation who would not be so whole-heartedly welcoming. There probably were a few parishioners for whom a couple like Ellen and me raised questions, maybe even some hostile feelings.

I felt a twinge of pain in my gut as I was reminded of the rejections we'd received from churches over the years—and especially from one particular church in Montana ten years ago. I had been a candidate to become their pastor. They had reviewed my resume and had invited me to meet the congregation and preach a sermon. I seemed to have the qualities and skills they were looking for to fill their pulpit. To my ever-hopeful eyes, they looked like a welcoming church!

Ellen and I were already mentally packing and moving to Montana when the phone rang. It was the chair of the search committee who told me, sadly, that they had voted not to offer me the opportunity to serve them. That church could not risk threats to their search committee members regarding the hiring of a lesbian pastor. I knew I would always carry with me the dull ache of yet another rejection. I certainly knew firsthand the pain of being designated "one of *them*," the "unacceptable."

Divisions between groups of people have always been with us. Who among us cannot think of at least one time when they heard someone say, "We don't want them in our bus, club, neighborhood, family or town"? Yet, I know from my own life experiences both the pain of separation and the jubilation in

14

reconciliation that comes when a connection—*un puente* (a bridge)—is made. An important part of my call has always been to facilitate the growth of new connections, to build new bridges, to bring people together, and to heal those divides.

Bridges have always fascinated me. Bridges were important in my growing up years. My hometown of Longview, Washington, is bordered by the Cowlitz and Columbia Rivers. Bridges were a part of every outing—to school, to church, to swim classes, to shop, to see fireworks on the lake. Every trip involved crossing a bridge. I own a poster that features a timber-pole bridge over a stream in a grove of redwoods that I love. I've carried it with me since my college days. It hung on a wall wherever I moved during my years as a teacher, and I had even put it up in my little upstairs office at the church in Belmont.

In fact, I wrote about becoming a "bridge minister" in my Theology of Ministry paper at the Pacific School of Religion. The assignment was to describe how I saw my role in God's work. At that time, I had no idea what it might really be like to be a "bridge minister," but I felt a call to become a connecting point, reconciling the people so often separated by age, gender, race, class, sexual orientation, language, education, mobility, political views, faith commitments, life experience or any of the ways by which some are seen as "outsiders" or "strangers." Many of us can empathize, having felt left out of one group or another, or isolated from the mainstream, at some time in our lives.

Even though we were newcomers to the area, Ellen and I felt at home right away in the lovely, historic Pescadero church. In fact, when we stepped into the soft, warm, golden light that shone through the sanctuary windows and reflected on the dark wood of the antique pews, we experienced a sense of "homecoming"—this place felt so familiar, so similar to other old sanctuaries in which we had worshipped before. It was even reminiscent of my grandparents' church in Medford, Oregon. There Grandpa had built the altar, the pulpit, and the pews in a style very much like the ones here. Even the air had that wonderful "old church" smell. But despite basking in the glow of the familiar, we were still the *recién llegadas* (newcomers), meeting a group of people who had known each other for decades.

When the last hymn was sung, we joined the others heading toward the fellowship hall, a room attached to the back of the sanctuary. It was a wainscoted, wood-toned, warm and friendly place with a good-sized kitchen visible at one side. That morning it seemed packed with people clutching coffee mugs and talking with their friends. Like any strangers, we felt a little left out—until one friendly-looking woman, noticing that we were new, walked over and urged us to help ourselves to coffee and cookies. "My name is Barbara," she said, "and I'd like to welcome you to Pescadero Community Church. Do you live around here?"

I introduced Ellen and myself, and told her about my teaching assignment with the recently arrived students at the high school. When she heard that I was teaching ESL classes, she called over another woman, Janet, and they told me about the ESL classes that *they* had been teaching, right there in the church, for more than a decade.

They described how in the mid-1980s there had been quite an increase in the number of immigrants coming from Mexico to look for work on the farms and ranches. The ease with which an individual made this journey, they said, had been much less daunting during that decade. Early on, they had offered the newcomers a chance to learn English, and fifteen to twenty Spanish-speaking men had faithfully come to the church to practice conversation right there in the fellowship hall. A few of them had even taken citizenship classes with Ray, a volunteer from the Half Moon Bay Episcopal church.

Janet chuckled as she told me that Ray had originally come to their church to sing in the choir. He loved to sing, and services in the Pescadero church started later on Sunday morning than did the ones in his own church in Half Moon Bay. It hadn't taken Barbara and Janet long to pick up on Ray's love of both languages and people—and to suggest that he offer citizenship coaching to their Spanish-speaking friends.

Unfortunately, only a handful of those who studied English at the church followed through with their citizenship applications.

As Barbara, Janet, Ray and a small cohort of volunteers worked with these newcomers, they began to develop some powerful personal connections. They learned that these men, ranging in age from teens to elders, had made the dangerous trip north across *la frontera* (the border) at great cost to work in the fields and nurseries around town. They learned that the men generally sent half of what they earned back to Mexico to support their families. And most poignantly, they learned that many of the men who had come north *sin sus familias* (without their families) felt enormously isolated and alone. For that reason, the trio began to refer to their new friends as "The Men Alone."

I was deeply drawn to the work that Barbara and Janet described that day, and I knew I wanted to become more involved. But they already did a great deal for The Men Alone—English classes, citizenship preparation. What more could I do?

It didn't take long to find out. A couple of weeks after we started attending the church, I bumped into Barbara at the Post Office.

"You're just the person I was hoping to see," she said. She explained that a young woman in her ESL class had come to her with a serious problem; and while she felt very well prepared to guide students in the use of English, she was not prepared to counsel this teenager on what was a deeply personal matter.

She explained that the young woman had long ago made a difficult personal choice, and now carried much *dolor y tristeza* (pain and sadness), along with *un miedo bien fuerte* (a dreadful fear) that she could no longer attend mass at the local church. Barbara asked if I would consider talking to a Catholic priest, perhaps someone outside of Pescadero, who would be willing to reassure her, absolve her, and then encourage her to return to mass? She added that she would arrange for me to meet with the young woman so that I could talk with her personally. This was clearly in the scope of my pastoral expertise.

The following day the young woman and I sat knee-to-knee in the tiny "office" in the back of the church sanctuary. She poured out her story in Spanish, trusting me since I seemed to be respected by her friend and teacher.

After she finished her story, I assured her that I would do my best to find a priest who was willing to absolve her. I told her that *le daría un mensaje a ella* (I would get a message to her) as soon as I had something to report. Once she had left, I turned to my address book. I skimmed through *los padres* (the priests) I had met working in the Interfaith Health Ministry program in San Mateo County, and began calling. After a few messages left, and calls back, I found a willing priest who worked nearby. He agreed to drive to Pescadero to meet with us. With some relief, I relayed the message to Barbara who called the troubled young woman.

On the following day, the priest and I met with the young woman. He heard her tearful confession and offered the words of absolution she longed to hear—while I prayed in the sanctuary in support. Together, as an ecumenical team of pastors, we bridged the differences in language and theology and brought peace to this young woman. It was a start. And reconciliation with God was the fruit of our labors. That day I saw how the new bridge I longed for might actually happen!

On weekdays, when I drove from *la escuela secundaria* (the high school) to *la iglesia* (the church), I began to catch glimpses of men in groups of two or three walking home from work or chatting at the local *taquería* (Mexican restaurant). I had not seen them at first because they moved as if clinging to the shadows. These guys knew how to be invisible!

The next time I saw one of these men on the street, I greeted him with a hello. Surprise flashed on his face. Here was *una huerita* (a white woman) with short, auburn hair who was speaking to him warmly—and she was near that church by the bridge, not their Catholic church!

In fact, I began spending Wednesdays after school and into the evening on the steps of the church—with its heavy, redwood front doors flung wide open—*asolándome* (sunning myself) on the porch. On many days, as a group of men walked or biked by, I would step out into the village street to greet them, shake their hands, and inquire about their workday and their families. They would often repond, *"¿Por qué me toca? Estoy tan mugroso* (Why would you touch me? I'm so gross, dirty)." And I would think to myself, we all are a part of the family here in the Pescadero Church. I'm just the offering the hand of friendship.

Although they were short in stature, and bronze-skinned, with very black hair and dark eyes, these men did not seem foreign to me. Neither were they unapproachable, for each face reminded me of the men that my mentor, the Rev. Dan Aprá, regularly shared worship and agape meals with back in Berkeley.

At his church, First Congregational of Berkeley, I met and ate with Spanish-speaking men and their families regularly during my seminary days, people who could have been relatives of these men. On those evenings, our dear friends from El Cerrito would go out to buy the best burritos in Hayward. They would drive as fast as they could through the late afternoon *tapones* (traffic) to bring those burritos hot and fragrant to the church, to be ready when our Spanish-speaking friends arrived. We would share that wonderful comfort food as we laughed and talked about what was happening in our lives. When the last crumb was gone, we would offer thanks for the blessings of that day: reading scripture, singing and praying together. Then Rev. Dan would offer communion around the table, an agape meal, and all of us would share what we were grateful for before we went our separate ways. Truly these were holy gatherings.

One of the first men to respond to *mis saludos* (my greetings) in that Pescadero street was Gabriel. He told me that he had worked in the fields and nurseries around the village for at least *quince años* (fifteen years) and was well into his middle years of life, like me.

He said that many of the men around town came from the state of Oaxaca (pronounced wa-HA-ka). These men were some of the most identifiably indigenous of Mexican nationals, shorter in stature, darker skinned, and the least literate. At home their families spoke one of the many living languages of the area. Scholars have recorded at least thirty-five (usually entirely) oral languages in the state of Oaxaca alone.

Most of these *trabajadores* (workers) probably never had the opportunity to attend school. If a man from that area was fortunate enough to go to school, he might have been able to attend only through the third grade. And over the years that I worked with these men from Mexico, I knew very few who were even that lucky. For most boys, the distance between their homes and a school, or the need to work in the fields with their families, kept them out of the classroom.

I had been taught in college that without an early foundation in basic literacy, it was nearly impossible for an adult to become literate—in either Spanish or English. Most of the men I would meet in Pescadero found it extremely hard to learn to speak even *un poquito* (a little) English.

Gabriel was my peer by age, experience, and faithful practices, and he seemed to know everyone in town. His side job, beyond being line boss of the *florería* (nursery), was to tend to the music teacher's home, pets and garden when she was visiting her family out of state. His good name and reputation was a model and fine reminder to townsfolk that *convivimos muy bien* (we all live together very well) in our community.

Gabriel told me that his wife and children lived in Mexico, and he had not been back for at least a decade. His infrequent calls home left him very much alone in Pescadero. We commiserated that both of us had a long trek home and could not see our families as often as we would like. He told me that he owned property in Mexico and had a business there. But his children were growing up without him, and he feared that his wife *casi no le conocía* (hardly knew him), since he had left for *el norte* (the North) in his thirties and was now in his late forties.

Gabriel also filled me in on the reasons many workers come North, as he had. Either their own land was "no good"— they could no longer grow *cosechas* (crops)—or there were very few full-time jobs that were *disponible* (available) in rural villages. If a man did get one of the few full-time jobs available, he might be paid as little as five dollars a day. Unfortunately, the cost of water alone would take about a third of that amount each day. As he sketched the details of life in his village, I began to realize that these solitary men were *economic* refugees.

I also learned that many of the workers from the countryside migrated to Mexico City, or other big cities, hoping for a chance at a job. Once these displaced workers arrived in any of Mexico's big cities, they found that there were no public restrooms, no school for the kids, and no housing for their families. At first they might sell whatever product or crafts they brought with them, but once these were gone, they had few options. Many of these folks were reduced to selling trinkets or flowers to tourists on the street. Gabriel told me that he had tried living in three different places in Mexico before arriving in California.

Later, when I visited Cuernavaca, Morelos, I talked with a man then living in *el barrio La Estación* (a neighborhood called the Train Station), where many displaced families ended up. He confided with sorrow the story of his brother's family after they moved to the city. It seems that the oldest child in the family was a seven-year-old boy, and not very big. His mother would go to the flower market early in the morning to select fresh *flores* (flowers) so that she could make up little bouquets to sell. The boy would then take the bouquets in *una canasta* (a basket) and try to sell them late into the evening to tourists visiting the city. It would be hard for any child, standing on a busy corner late at night, to approach strangers and be rudely pushed aside or ignored, but he did it.

One night after he had sold all his *rosas* (roses) and had *una bolsa de pesos* (a bag of pesos) to take back to his mother, he headed for home. On the way, four older boys jumped him, took his money, beat him badly, and left him lying in the dirt.

It is hard for us to imagine the struggles families go through to survive; yet, I am convinced that too many families endure such incidents and suffering, over and over. It is little wonder that so many able-bodied adults make the risky trip north to support *los queridos* (their loved ones).

Back on the streets of Pescadero, Gabriel introduced me to his friends Carlos, Luz, and Mauricio. In the weeks that followed, we often talked on the steps of the church, or sat together on *los bancos* (the benches) in the Peace Park at the crossroads. This tiny plaza, in front of *el correo* (the post office), had been created several years ago by the Peace Committee of our church. They had planted a small flower garden that brightened the corner. *El letrero* (the community message board) was also there, visible to everyone.

Later, over coffee, I told Margaret about these developments. I described how important this plaza-like "center of town" was. And I explained that because most of Pescadero's mail is delivered to *apartados* (individual boxes) at the post office, almost everyone in town shows up there to pick up their mail.

"What about good old RFD—rural free delivery?" she asked, remembering her childhood growing up in Iowa.

"Well, there are those who do get their mail delivered to homes and ranches," I responded, "but even if your mail gets delivered, you still have to come in to buy stamps, purchase money orders, make copies and pick up packages." It was not uncommon for several people to share a post office box, and the traffic across the plaza was constant.

The plaza also featured the town flagpole, where the flag flew each day. When someone died, the flag was dropped to *media hasta* (half-mast) and a notice was posted on the entrance to the mailbox room. The spot was *el corazón verdadero* (the real heart) of our town.

On weekdays from 8 a.m. to 4 p.m., I was with my high school classes. These teen-agers, with their raging hormones, were quite a challenge to me after fifteen years of not teaching school. I was assigned a couple of sections of Spanish, two of English, and one of English as a Second Language (ESL) made up of students recently arrived from Mexico.

Like any veteran teacher, I began the school year by creating a seating chart. In my previous classes, I had asked students to take their seats in a particular order to help me learn their names. They sat where I placed them, not always gracefully or happily, but generally obediently. For most of them, it rarely seemed to matter where they sat.

Not true with my new students! When I tried to impose seating charts on these students, I was abruptly reminded of the many cultural divisions among people from Mexico. Students who came from a one particular region of Mexico would often toss *chispas* (feisty words) at students from a feuding region or family. Here was another place where bridges were needed— bridges that would allow each young person to maintain the self-respect and honor that he or she had developed through family origins and sibling order while in the company of students from other areas.

Among our *recién llegados* (recent arrivals) at the school was a young woman called Martina. She had arrived in Pescadero to live with her parents just days before the high school term started. That first morning of class, she sank into her seat stoic and silent, with tears streaming down her face. She would not speak to me, and I had no clue as to what her distress might be. But I was determined to find out.

The one person who had a finger on the pulse of the school—and who knew everything about everyone in it—was Socorro, the school secretary. In the course of her job, she learned who was from where, and why each student was coming to this school at this time. Obviously, I needed her insight.

Socorro told me that when Martina's parents had immigrated to California many years earlier, she, as the eldest child, had chosen to stay in Mexico to live with and care for her *abuela* (grandmother). During the summer just past, her grandmother *se murió* (had died), and relatives in Mexico had arranged for Martina to rejoin her family in Pescadero and complete high school in the United States. Sitting in my class, Martina was deep in mourning.

Her grief, so real and understandable, was compounded by a frightening new school experience. She knew no English, and she had been placed in classes in *ciencia*, *historia*, y *matemática* (science, history and math) where no instruction was given in Spanish. It was true that some peer tutors were available for Spanish-speaking students, but all too often their pride kept them from accepting help. She knew that she would have to pass all her classes to graduate, but the ESL class that I taught was the only place where she heard anything that she could understand! It was not surprising that she wept—not only out of grief, but also at the futility of her situation. Her plight was in stark contrast to her younger sister, who had proven to be an excellent student and who had graduated with honors the year before.

For all these reasons Martina continued to resist many people's efforts to help. Sadly, her experience in school did not improve much during that year; and when June came she "graduated" without many of the basic skills she might have gained had that year been different.

During the following week, I shared Martina's story with Margaret. I also described my first parent-teacher conferences.

"How do the teachers handle conferences with Spanish-speaking parents, since many of these parents probably won't understand what the teachers say?" she asked.

I told her that since we had no other bilingual teachers in Pescadero High, the faculty relied on bilingual students, who were expected to serve as "personal bridges" in confidential translations for their own parents. I was the only teacher who spoke directly to the parents in Spanish.

Having children translate for their parents is not ideal, but it was necessary at the time. Like children of deaf parents, our bilingual students reported their own progress to their parents. When the occasion arose, they would also translate between their parents and the *bomberos* (firefighters or emergency medical personnel) who aided our community in a crisis. Everyone knew it was not ideal for a child to translate for a parent or sibling in crisis. But it was expedient, and so for a time it was done.

"But you know, Margaret, I did meet every single one of my students' Spanish-speaking parents," I told her. In fact, I found these mothers and fathers eager to support their students, whether sons or daughters. They rushed from work to school to meet with teachers they could not understand and who did not understand them, and the kids did their best to translate. What a challenge! Years later, we trained a group of high school students in how to talk to other students' parents and how to practice confidentiality. This freed children from the responsibility of translating for their own parents and preserved the confidentiality of those meetings.

I tried to describe to Margaret the great divide that lack of a common language, experience, and culture can create. I saw how it divided these various groups of people sharing the same local area. I also saw how people of good will could work together to overcome that gap *de dos lados* (from both sides). I told her of my longing to somehow establish a working bridge. She listened, understanding what I was saying.

"What's the word for 'bridge' in Spanish?" she asked.

"*Puente,*" I responded. My favorite image! I sensed that the foundation of a new bridge—a connection—was beginning to be laid.

Fue un milagro (it was a miracle) that shortly after we had this conversation, I heard about a personal trust fund that would later become a resource for funding our outreach ministry. An individual whose family had taken an interest in farm workers had set aside seed money to initiate a program to help those workers. This person appreciated the United Church of Christ's position on faithfulness to the prophetic vision of *peace with justice* in our everyday lives, and wanted to cultivate multicultural churches and communities. To further this vision, the donor had pledged thirty thousand dollars, to be awarded in ten-thousand-dollar-a-year increments, over a three-year period. If I could secure this gift, it would enable me to propose to the church that they sponsor a new outreach ministry.

25

I dashed out to see our senior pastor, the Reverend Orril, in his rustic cabin in Loma Mar. Breathlessly, I told him about the money and my dream. He beamed at me, his crinkling eyes bright with excitement. He told me that he had felt for a long time that such a program had been needed, but the church hadn't had the resources to support it. Now there was hope.

Together we drafted a proposal that anchored the bridge ministry to the church. It specified that I would work five hours a week in pastoral service and five hours a week in outreach ministry with the workers, for a total of a quarter-time pastoral position with benefits. Later when Orril took this proposal to the whole congregation, they enthusiastically voted to add $5,000 to the seed money. Now there was $15,000 a year to fund these pastoral hours, plus benefits, and enough money left over to supply items that might be needed in the new ministry. This was the firm foundation on which we could build our bridge. It was a critical *primer paso* (first step).

Pescadero Community Church had never had an official agreement with anyone to provide pastoral services, so it was a new beginning for them as a congregation, too.

As a pastor, I knew that a "pastoral relations committee" would be essential to the work of the minister. Every active pastor needs a group of confidential, knowledgeable people to provide advice, feedback, and support. Fortunately, I had several such people in mind, and I quickly convened a new "Puente Advisory Committee." These dear friends would prove to be invaluable allies as the ministry expanded.

For some time, people in church had referred to the workers I'd befriended as "Wendy's Guys." But once the congregation approved our agreement, once we officially started offering our compassionate response of radical hospitality, we began to call this outreach *"Puente* (Bridge) Ministry."

3

Pausing to Listen

Listening is an attitude of the heart,
a genuine desire to be with another
which both attracts and heals.

— J. Isham

Driving along the coast to work each morning that first year, I began to notice the fields along the highway. They grew brown during late summer and fall, only to be transformed with the first rains of winter into lush shades of green. I watched the hawks wheeling overhead, egrets fishing for their breakfasts, and a myriad of other wonderful birds I couldn't name. Fortunately, I had on my bookshelf a *Sibley's Field Guide to Birds* and I took to carrying it in the car, stopping from time to time to look up a sighting. For me each bird was a reminder of God's graceful presence in all of my life.

Birds weren't the only interesting new creatures along my path. There were often cyclists puffing up the hills, and sometimes there were older people driving along in small campers. I usually smiled and waved. Some days I'd catch a friendly wave back. I loved these glimpses of other travelers as I rode along.

One day I saw a man, a slight character, ambling with his walking stick along my commute. At first I thought he might be another of the field workers like those I was meeting on the streets of Pescadero as part of the new Puente Ministry. But there was something different about this man. Sometimes he would be walking from Santa Cruz toward Pescadero, other times he would be strolling along the other side of the road apparently headed for Half Moon Bay. If I caught his eye, I'd raise my hand in a friendly greeting, and sometimes he waved back.

Weeks went by when I didn't see him at all; but one morning I happened to spot him just at that point on the highway where I would normally turn off onto Pescadero Creek Road and cruise into town. There's plenty of room right there to pull off the highway, so I did. As I stepped out of the car I called to him, "Good Morning! How are you today?"

His face cracked into a smile, and he walked hesitantly toward me. We talked for a minute or two, and he told me he was called "Johnnie Angel," but it was clear that he was anxious to be off. Certainly here was a colorful character, a solitary man, but obviously not one of the local workers. As we talked he was not unfriendly at all, but wary and a bit skittish. I did not want to alarm him, so that first day I quietly got back into to my car and went on into work.

Almost daily now as I went back and forth from the high school to the church, I stopped to chat with the men on the street. I was also meeting and talking with long-time community folks, the townspeople. It wasn't long until I began hearing about the Pescadero Municipal Advisory Council or PMAC (Pee-Mack). This was the local government of our little unincorporated historical *aldea* (village) of Pescadero, and it worked in concert with the regional county supervisor to govern and support our community.

At about this time, the Council became very concerned over a story circulating around town. According to the *chisme* (rumors), a Mexican man had raped an Anglo woman while she was out jogging!

Fortunately, the same day I heard this rumor, I also heard the real story from that same woman, the alleged victim, who happened to be a church member. We had been chatting casually about potential rental properties and other town news, and this rumor came up. She assured me that she was indeed the woman in the story, but she had not been physically attacked at all. She had only heard *piropos* (cat calls) from a man as he followed her down the street.

Latin men often *tiran piropos* (toss out comments) about passing women. This may be accepted or customary in parts of Mexico, but it was certainly not welcome or expected in Pescadero. Therefore, it is not surprising that this cultural misunderstanding coupled with the lone woman jogger's perceived feeling of vulnerability had quickly escalated this incident into rumors of a serious criminal offense!

I told this story to Margaret.

"How is any newcomer from another culture to know how to behave, or what the 'silent expectations' might be in the Pescadero community?" I asked.

¡No pudo ser (it was impossible)! While Pescadero residents certainly had expectations about public behavior, there was no attempt to convey those expectations to outsiders. There were no written rules about how much noise was acceptable, and there was no stated curfew for young people. None of us who were new to the community could know when we had crossed over the line. Clearly, it was time to spell out those unspoken expectations.

I proposed that a guide sheet be created which would clarify the accepted practices of our communal life in the Pescadero. I was encouraged to approach various community leaders to collaborate with me on the creation, translation, and legal clarity of such a sheet. I chose Sheriff Lt. John; Latina pre-school teacher, Norka; and Dr. Velia, a longtime community activist and San Francisco State University professor, who had come to our town as an advocate for migrant education during the legal battles for equal education in Pescadero. They all agreed that a guide sheet was needed.

As we began to talk, I remember asking, "How else might a man from Mexico know that playing music after 10 p.m.

29

could be considered an offense?" When I lived and worked as a VISTA volunteer in Puerto Rico, music pulsed through the streets into the wee hours without anyone protesting. It was *una celebración y gratitud para el regalo de la vida cada día* (a celebration of, and gratitude for, the gift of life)!

Clearly, now was time for a bilingual *informe* (listing) of this community's expectations, limits, and consequences regarding activities such as playing music, driving too fast through town, making comments about women, relieving oneself on the street, and drinking in public. Our little *junta* (group) met many times for nearly a year, and we talked with everyone in the community who was interested. Finally, we summarized the key ideas on a single sheet of paper. We agreed to title our new document *"Para el Bienestar de la Comunidad* (for the Well-Being of the Community)."

We had a draft printed on astrobright green paper. When we presented it to the PMAC, they were delighted. They passed it on to the San Mateo County Board of Supervisors, the oversight and governing body for our unincorporated town, who added their approval and even paid for the printing. Copies of the Green Sheet were given to every newcomer we met. The public schools sent this information home with each student; and the local taquería, the post office, and Duarte's restaurant were all given an ample supply.

During these months as I was getting acquainted in the area and working on the Green Sheet, I met the couple who had for several years staffed the Coastside Catholic Worker House. Because of their strong faith and spiritual practice, Kathy and Mike had left their lucrative jobs as nurse and accountant to follow this call to minister. They offered me a tour around Half Moon Bay and the neighboring agricultural region, telling me about their experiences serving the poorest of the poor, and I realized they shared my vision. A friendship grew between us, and they began to mentor me. We were like *hermanos espirituales* (spiritual siblings). And as the years went on, we would share resources from time to time. If they had a good supply of *pañales* (diapers) and we were out, they brought us diapers. If we had extra *bolsas* (sleeping bags), or *comestibles* (groceries), and they were in need, we drove up with a load.

But what became most important to me was the kindred spirit we shared during our impromptu, ecumenical house-church gatherings. Serving in outreach ministries can be lonely. We are sent what we need by our sustaining Creator.

About the same time, I met Fátima and Guillermo at the Coastside Opportunity Center (known now as Coastside Hope), also in Half Moon Bay. These dedicated folks contributed much to my understanding of how it was to be a resource for the Mexican workers on the Coast. We found we had common areas of concern and shared what we had discovered about people who were available for referrals, and special programs that extended their services to Pescadero and further south along the coast. No sense in reinventing the wheel!

With my growing involvement with The Men Alone, and my daily activities with people in Pescadero, I found my *corazón* (heart) and *espíritu* (spirit) had taken root in town. It became urgent for my whole being to find a place nearby. I needed to be "here" where my *alma* (soul) was.

The home that Ellen and I shared twenty-two miles north of Pescadero in Half Moon Bay was way too far from the action. I wanted to be somewhere within a two-mile radius of town. Buying a house was out of the question: listings in town started at about $700,000, well out of our price range. What's more, we had decided that we were through with owning property in California; we really preferred renting. But rentals were few and far between in the circle that included Stage Road, North Street, and Pescadero Creek Road. Maybe I could count a hundred living units in all, and very few of them were ever for rent.

I continued looking for a place for us to live while I was working on the Green Sheet. Daily as I talked with people about their expectations for appropriate behavior in town, I mentioned that we would like to move into the area, but hadn't been able to find a place to rent. People assured me that they would keep their ears open and get back to me if they heard of anything.

It wasn't long before I was told that the first house on Pescadero Creek Road, "the flood house" by the bridge where Butano Creek joins Pescadero Creek, might be available. That word came to us from the very woman jogger whose encounter had triggered the Green Sheet. News travels fast in a small community—and this time, it was to our advantage.

We jumped at this opportunity. We agreed that we should lease the recently remodeled 1920s cottage despite the fact that it sat right on a bank at the confluence of two creeks. It was simply too good to pass up.

We understood that this house was on the local flood plain. We could see the village's three-foot-tall floodwater marker on the road adjacent to the property. Folks who lived nearby told us that this flood marker was designed to indicate whether it was safe to pass in those times when high water rushed from the creeks, over the fields, onto the marsh, and out to the Pacific Ocean. Everyone made sure we knew the risks. They even described how the California Fire Department set up roadblocks and sandwich board warnings.

Nevertheless, the bungalow was picturesque and held a certain charm for us. It would be delightful in the beautiful spring, summer, and dry mid-winter. We rushed to put down our deposit and sign the papers. Then, of course, we had to wait. When the remodeling was finished and it was ready, friends from both our former and new churches helped us move from Princeton Harbor in Half Moon Bay to Pescadero.

This tiny cottage was almost half the size of our home in Princeton Harbor, so we gave away or donated items we no longer needed. I did insist on bringing my piano, our computers, the TV, our bed and favorite chairs and couch, but a lot of other stuff went to the thrift shop. This was the first of several downsizing, shedding times, as we reached for a simpler life. Finally, we brought in the last box and hung up the last shirt.

Now I could walk or bike to the church, to school, to the beach, or to the post office. Ellen, bless her heart for the sake of this ministry, had an even longer commute—about thirty miles one-way—a reality that she handled with grace for the next five years.

But we had crossed over! With her *don* (gift) to me of two to three hours daily on the road, she allowed us to be grounded in the village, far from the urban services, entertainment, sprawl, pace, and population of the Bay Area. Now we were established as local residents. I was teaching in the local high school and preaching every few weeks as part of the group of volunteer ministers. I was committed to Pescadero and to The Men Alone, *nuestros hermanos* (our brothers).

It wasn't long until our casual conversations at the Peace Park and on the street became a little more formalized. I told the men I would definitely be on the front steps of the church every Wednesday afternoon when they came into town from work. As the resident bilingual pastor, I offered Bible study and prayer there as well as conversation and confidential counsel.

When I described these Wednesday meetings to the women at a Ladies' Guild lunch, they suggested that they might buy some Bibles in Spanish. At that time, we all imagined that my contact with the men would be focused on their spiritual life, on starting bilingual services, and on regular visitations. This is the kind of thing pastors usually do. And so I began offering bilingual Bibles and sharing simple prayers. Whatever we happened to talk about, the men's comments were sprinkled with affirmations of their faith: "*Si Dios quiera* (if God wishes)" or "*Primero Dios* (we'll see what God has in mind first)." These living creeds resonated in their hearts. How fully faithful they were! What lessons they could teach me and our community about daily commitment, trust, faith, and hope in God!

With the potential for such an intimate connection between souls, I made a point of asking each man's name so that I could greet him with it. This practice of learning people's names, and *remembering* them, is central to both my teaching and pastoral mindset. It is rooted in Scripture: "I have called you by name, and you are mine."[4] I felt a poignant call to be

---

[4] Isaiah 43:1b

certain no one felt "other" again in our village, and all would indeed be called by name.

Traditionally Spanish family names are not formed like English family names. We are accustomed to a first, middle, and last name—with the last name most often that of one of our parents. The pattern in Mexico often involves using various first and saints' names along with a compound family name from both the mother's and father's side. In the transition from Mexico to the United States, some men had picked up *apodos* (nicknames), too. I loved being able to link names with faces at last. As a teacher I had always warmed to the idea of learning my students' names quickly, and now that skill was transferred to my pastoral care with new friends.

The men not only told me their names but also taught me some of their oral languages—Chatino, Nahuatl, and Tepec. They gave me *las palabras del las piezas de una bici, chuparosa, mariposas, y flores* (the words for bike parts, hummingbirds, butterflies, and flowers). Although Spanish was their working language, their native tongues were often those indigenous, unwritten languages. Our conversations were always crossing back and forth from *español al inglés* (Spanish to English). "*¿Cómo se dice ... en inglés o español* (how do you say ... in English or Spanish)?" We often talked way past dark on *los miércoles* (most Wednesdays).

From these conversations, I learned how the men felt about their lives in Pescadero. I heard quite often one particular *dicho* (saying): "*Llegamos como una piedra en un pozo* (we were dropped like a rock into a well)." Here they stayed, on occasion traveling to Watsonville to a *lavandería* (laundromat) or a family *fiesta* (celebration), but usually simply waiting on the ranch for their next opportunity to work.

I also found out that there were few *baños públicos* (public bathrooms) and literally no place for the men who did not have adequate housing to clean up or do laundry. Little wonder that they used the hidden corners as latrines. Soon there was a little more comfort and welcome for them as the church installed a porta-potty in its parking lot. Another was placed in town near a store, and that helped a little. La Taquería de Los Amigos also allowed the men to use their indoor restroom. Here they could run a little water to wash their hands and faces. Still, no place in town offered a public drinking fountain that would allow our brothers to get a drink of water. It is hard for me to imagine a town where I would have no appropriate place to go to the bathroom, no place to wash my hands, and no place to get a drink of water! These conveniences are available to me as a customer, but for the men they were non-existent. A wake-up call for me!

I continued to be astonished at the invisibility of our brothers in town. Recently arrived *jovencitos* (younger men) often slept wherever they could find a little shelter from the elements. A few youthful workers held out for "campsites" where they felt secure and didn't have to pay rent—and some slept in friends' cars or abandoned sheds. Some bedded down on a partly covered dirt ledge under the Stage Road Bridge just across the church's parking lot. We'd often notice cardboard and clothes tightly stashed in the crevasses under that bridge—until the El Niño flood of 1998 washed it out. Once these men were hired on, they could move into *vivienda* (worker housing) at the farms or nurseries.

Wherever they might sleep, these faith-filled men seemed to be living out the scripture in Matthew which reminds us to trust that God who clothes and cares for the wildflowers surely will take good care of us, too:

> If God gives such attention
> To the appearance of wildflowers—
> Most of which are never even seen—
> Don't you think God will attend to you,
> Take pride in you, do the best for you?
> What I'm trying to do here is to get you to relax,
> To not be so preoccupied with getting,
> So you can respond to God's giving.
> People who don't know God
> And the way God works

Fuss over these things,
But you know both God and how God works.
Steep your life in God-reality,
God-initiative,
God-provisions.
Don't worry about missing out.
You'll find all your everyday human concerns
will be met.

—Matthew 6:29-31, *The Message*

I noticed early on that the men usually wore dark or black sweatshirts and jeans. These colors were chosen not because they were *de moda* (fashionable), but simply because they were easier to keep clean. Keeping clean was a major challenge. Later, I would learn that at least half of the workers' housing didn't have convenient places to wash clothes. Any washing machines that *were* accessible washed with cold water only, and none had dryers.

At home the men had relied on women in their families—*esposas, hermanas, tías, abuelas, o novias* (wives, sisters, aunts, grandmothers or girlfriends)—to care for them, to do their laundry, to make sure they had something healthy and good to eat, and to provide companionship. Here, while they became our *hermanos* (brothers), they were still alone, and they had to learn how to handle these day-to-day tasks for themselves in a strange land.

Living in the rough as they did, they had no *sala* (living room) just to sit around in after work. Neither was there anyone to relax with or talk to in a house of *desconocidos* (strangers). If they had on-site housing in *baracas o trailas* (barracks or trailers), they probably lived four men to a room in two sets of bunk beds, or twelve in a room dormitory-style. Sometimes they were housed eight together in a garage. Although these places were relatively warm and dry, none of them was conducive to easy socializing, nor was there any private space for *reflección*

(Sabbath time), or a *siesta* (nap). And there definitely was no place to share a confidential conversation.

When a man was hired on at a ranch, he usually had a place to sleep. But even with that relative sense of security, he always knew that he lacked the proper papers to be in this country and he might be *agarrado* (picked up) at any time. Fortunately, our San Mateo County Sheriff's Lieutenant had declared that he would not cooperate with the Immigration and Naturalization Service (INS), then known as *"La Migra"* when those officers elected to make random sweeps. Rather, he would tenderly joke about the situation, referring to Pescadero as "Péxico." Nor would he allow those officers to pick up workers in our part of the county "for being brown" as long as the men stayed out of trouble with the law. His was an official voice invoking the memory of "sanctuary" offered to Salvadoran refugees in the '80s. Such a voice echoes in too few states today as the issue of immigrant status takes prominence in the news.

If a man bought *un chueco* (a fake) Social Security card with nine numbers, and if it were assigned to his name, he seemed to be able to work here unless he broke the law. His employer deducted Social Security from his pay and sent it in as he would have had the number been legitimately the worker's own. The employer recorded the number on his employment sheets showing he was in compliance. During those years the authorities seemed to accept this deception without comment. It broke my heart to know that while I would be able to draw on those very funds when I retired, the men who had paid into the system could never stop working.

However, if *un trabajador* (a worker) received a DUI or a moving violation or was charged with a felony, he was "in the system," and a free ride home across the border was the cost of the first offense. The potential for incurring that kind of violation loomed every time a man got behind the wheel of a car.

Up until about 1993 or 1994 state laws allowed for Mexican nationals to get driver's licenses and insurance while living in this country. But by the time our ministry began in

Pescadero, these perks were no longer available to the men. And for that reason, they had no idea what the rules of the road were here. Add a bit of alcohol to that picture and you can easily see why driving a car could result in hasty deportation, and might sometimes be life threatening! Early on, I realized that driving a car was not a wise mode of transportation for these men, and most of these laborers seemed to understand that, too. Generally, they walked everywhere.

With all that hassle, I wondered why they didn't just get a permit to work here before they came. It seemed so obvious. There must be rules, but surely once the forms had been filled out, that would be that. I made some inquiries. Very quickly I discovered that no regular work visas were available to Mexicans wanting to work in the U.S. except those for a job requiring a particular skill, such as the H-2 permit for horse training.[5] Some of the men also told me stories of friends in Mexico who had tried to apply for work permits, giving substantial sums of money to government officials, attorneys, or priests who said they would file the papers for them. Weeks later, they found that their money was gone and they were no closer to getting a permit. When you need to earn money *día tras día* (day after day) to feed your family, you really can't wait years! This made unauthorized border crossing an economic necessity.

I also discovered that for a Mexican worker living in the U.S. and applying for citizenship, the backlog of applications in U.S. Immigration Services produced a wait-time of up to eight years. What's more, while a person is in the waiting period, he is

---

[5] The H-2 program operated alongside the Bracero program (1942-1964), which allowed farmers along the Eastern seaboard to import Jamaican and other foreign workers to hand-cut sugar cane in Florida and pick apples in the Northeast. Farm employers who employed H-2 workers, like those operating under the Bracero program, had to convince the U.S. Department of Labor that U.S. workers were unavailable at government-set wages and to provide the foreign workers with free housing and contracts that spelled out their rights and responsibilities.

not allowed to cross into Mexico and return to the United States. Any sort of legal status seemed to be out of reach. [6]

Each Wednesday night as I continued *charlar* (to chat) with these men, I learned more. I heard stories of men who walked or rode bikes to the fields or nurseries along the Pacific Coast Highway via narrow two-lane roads through hills and canyons. They traveled in the dawn and dusk hours when visibility was poor, and from time to time a man would be injured or killed on those roads.

What more could Puente Ministry do *para servirles* (to serve) these men? Could we at least help them become more visible while they walked along the roads and highway?

Reflectors would certainly make them easier to see!

The next time Ellen and I drove over the hill to shop in San Mateo, I searched several big sporting goods stores for reflectors. At that time there wasn't a big selection, but I did find a few reflectors that were mounted on leg bands. Sad to say, they were designed for use by touring bikers in spandex attire. When I brought them back to Pescadero and asked the younger men to try them, the leg bands didn't stretch enough to fit over their heavy, rubber barn boots. Next I tried stick-on reflective-tape patches, but they didn't stick to either the rubber boots or the *traje de ule* (rubber rain slickers and pants) the men wore during the rainy season.

Finally, Rich—the owner of the bike shop in Half Moon Bay—found us a source for reflectors that would clip onto shirts, jackets and baseball caps. They were just the right shape and size, and required two small batteries. All I had to do was convince the men to wear them!

One Wednesday evening I persuaded a couple of younger men to try them on. We took their pictures to show how the reflectors made them easier to see. But a month or so later they both told me that the ongoing cost of batteries was prohibitive.

We did not give up. I told them, "*No quiero concocerle y después enterrarle* (I don't want to learn your name and be the

---

[6] http://www.us-immigration.com

officiant at your funeral)." I pleaded with them to protect themselves from the cars that "*no les hacen caso* (do not pay any attention to you)." Some of the younger men did accept my invitation to wear a reflector that first season. And many of the reflectors were sent home to children in Mexico, too. This was not such a bad ministry either: I was to come to understand that these are solid family men who will protect their children first and foremost. A great model for all families!

Finally, one day a young man said, "*¡Sí, gracias, pero, no tengo ni bici* (yes, thank you, but I don't have a bike)!" That comment started a whole new chapter in our fledgling ministry.

4

Meeting The Men Alone

Ours is not the task of
fixing the entire world all at once,
but of stretching out to mend
the part of the world that is within our reach.

— Clarissa Pinkola Estés, PhD
*"Letter To A Young Activist During Troubled Times:
Do Not Lose Heart, We Were Made For These Times"*

Bikes! Obviously, we needed bikes! What a natural solution. Biking would be a much easier, safer, more efficient, and comfortable mode of transportation than walking. The light dawned as I sat eating lunch with Margaret, bemoaning the plight of the workers with their perilous walks on the highway's edge added to long days of fieldwork. I had heard that deaths were regularly recorded, but all too often it was impossible to find the name of the deceased. Even if a name were known, there was no record of next of kin; so, no one would be notified in Mexico. When I told Margaret about the young man who wanted a reflector but had no bike, it all clicked. The men really needed better transportation! We would get bikes for them to ride.

Driving cars was not really a good option for any of these workers. Although some men came with a driver's license from Mexico—or from Washington or Oregon or another state that offered them, that license was legal for only one year. And worse yet, after it expired, the driver was not legally able to replace it with one from California.

Immigrant workers who are Mexican nationals are still not eligible for driver's licenses in California as of this writing. It is not only the men who are affected by this, but also the mothers who needed to drive their children to school and to get to work themselves. I quickly learned that this situation meant that parents living out on the ranches had no choice but to drive without a license. Of course, if anyone accepted a job outside the *aldea* (village) of Pescadero, he or she ran the great risk of being arrested during a routine traffic stop—even for a broken tail light. And always there was the fear of being stopped for "driving while brown." Both encounters with the law could result in immediate deportation. Bikes, on the other hand, required no licenses or insurance and were definitely faster and more comfortable than walking. Rainy weather was the biggest drawback, but workers never complained.

"Why not see if anyone we know has any unused bikes in their garage? I know we do," Margaret suggested. Her no-longer-used bikes were stuffed in the back of our truck, as were a few from Bob and Ella Mae, Bob and Lois, and other friends at our old Belmont church. Ellen and I also bought bikes for a few dollars when we saw them at garage sales in the area. It seemed that there were bikes to be had all over! Thus, it became a process of gleaning. A bicycle that someone no longer wanted would become a treasured possession for a man who truly needed it to get and maintain a job.

By this time, Ellen and I were settled into our house by the bridge on Pescadero Creek Road. Fortunately, our new home came with access to an outbuilding, which we quickly filled with bikes and extra bike parts. *Estas bicis* (these bikes) were mostly good old three-speeds with decent seats. You know the kind. They were out of style, but really just right for the men. Even the unisex bikes proved to be very usable as the men often found them more comfortable! Their legs did not quite stretch enough to allow them to sit comfortably on the seats of the men's bikes and still reach the pedals or to dismount with comfort. Some of the men had never ridden a bike before, but they quickly learned. As these men grew accustomed to having a bike, they discovered that it served not only for "commuting" but also for service in the fields. When it was time to relocate long irrigation pipes from one area to another, they would bike thru the huge, muddy fields between newly planted rows, from one site to another, which could be literally miles.

I began to mention our need for used bikes to everyone I met. And once the flow of bikes started, it soon flooded our shed. It was amazing how many people responded! Could it be that many former bike-riders, now approaching middle age (like us), were enjoying less energetic leisure activities?

We haunted garage sales and picked up bikes for ten or twelve dollars. They went into the back of Ellen's red truck, which we'd named "Bing" for its cherry color, of course. Margaret created and posted a sign in the window of her shop asking for bike donations, and several came to us that way. News about the new Puente Ministry out in Pescadero spread throughout the network of churches in our conference, too. I was asked to conduct *talleres* (workshops) describing Puente's ministry during the annual meeting that spring—and people who heard me heeded my plea for bikes.

The San Lorenzo and Pleasant Hill United Church of Christ churches took the quest for bikes very seriously and began collecting them in large numbers, as did the people of the Berkeley church. One good source for bikes was the RV and bike-rental business. They recycled many bicycles and safety vests for us, and volunteers from the San Lorenzo church brought them to Pescadero. The Belmont church and Trinity Presbyterian church of San Carlos even invited us to preview their rummage sale for usable bicycles. *Corría la palabra* (the word was definitely getting around). Bikes rolled in. Here was a simple, concrete way that faithful, caring people could improve the daily life of agricultural workers, and they were eager to do it!

One day when our shed was full, a worker came to our home to pick up a bike for himself. I persuaded him to accept a second bike for *su hermano* (his brother). We even threw in an extra *llanta* (tire)! He was jubilant, and so was I. With the two bikes in tow, he happily sauntered home, walking along the edge of Pescadero Creek Road. He hadn't gone very far when he heard an ominous siren. A sheriff's deputy pulled up behind him, stopped and got out.

Not surprisingly, the deputy spoke to him in English.

"Hey! Where'd you get those bikes?"

Trembling, the man dropped both bikes and the tire, and scrambled to clasp both hands behind his head.

This was my own error! *No me dió cuenta* (it had never occurred to me) that The Men Alone were not trusted by others as I trusted them. I regarded each one as a brother in and out of our home. But this deputy did not share my faith in humanity, and he was not bilingual enough to get to the truth.

Instead, the officer frisked the worker, took his "phony" papers, and pocketed them! Would our friend lose his job when he asked to get off work to go to San Francisco or Watsonville and pay fifty to a hundred dollars for another *chueco* (fake) social security card? Without a card, no one would hire him. Then the deputy tossed the bikes into the back of his vehicle, and sent the man on his way with a stern warning. Since this took place just a short distance from my house, the frightened worker retraced his steps and told me what had happened. I insisted that he sit with me for a bit, have a cold drink of water, and we'd figure out what to do next.

I called Sheriff Lt. John and explained how I had given this worker the bikes and would be giving out many more bikes as part of the new Puente Ministry. Then I asked him, hesitantly, if he could return the man's papers. He told me it would be easy to return the bikes, but those fake papers were lost forever.

The next day Sheriff Lt. John showed up with the bikes. He was also carrying an engraver so that we could mark all the donated bikes with:

8-8-98, *la fecha* (the date)
PCC, (Pescadero Community Church)
don de Dios (a gift from God)

By using the engraver, each man receiving a bike would know that his bike was not to be sold, and no one could wrongly accuse him of stealing a bike ever again. I would make it clear that the bikes were to be passed on to others when a man no longer needed his.

The Lieutenant acknowledged that if I had been pushing two bikes and carrying a tire along the side of the road, the officer would have offered me a ride home. If it were I, there would have been no assumptions about an illegal action. But one of the men doing exactly the same thing was in a different category. He was "walking while brown." It was a painful reminder of my own white privilege. Puente Ministry also learned an important lesson that day: be sure to share details about our new activities and programs with all community agencies.

Later, telling Margaret about the incident, I was reminded of Romans 12:4-5, where Paul, the writer, describes how we are many in the body of Christ: we don't all have the same jobs, but we are needed by one another as members of one body. The same holds true for people who live in a small community. We each have different roles to play, but we must play those roles in harmony with each other for the good of the whole community.

This new connection with Lt. John became a long-lasting and positive one. Later that same month, he offered me a truckload of bikes from the county's lost & found in Redwood City. He told me that the clerk at the Sheriff's substation who oversaw the county's auctions of unclaimed items was passionately vigilant over *las sobras* (the leftovers) from that auction. When John told him about the need for bikes in Pescadero, this guy "discovered" dozens of unclaimed bikes for us. He arranged to have them delivered to the Montara substation, not far away, where we could pick them up.

Many others joined in the task of gathering up bikes for the workers. Several churches in the East Bay loaded up a moving van and several personal trucks with bikes and brought them over. SamTrans, the local bus service, gave us bikes from their lost & found. And when we checked with Stanford University, they told us that their unclaimed bikes went to Juvenile Hall in San Jose where they were put in running order by young men, many of whom were Latino themselves. Some of these bikes were offered to Puente, too.

Right from the beginning of the bike distribution, we were blessed to have a group of men offer their services to repair those bikes that still needed work when they arrived. Among those who handled such repairs was a high school youth who serviced bikes for a whole year to earn his community service hours. Another trusted repairman, Ed, who drove for the Old Jackson Nursery, brought rummage sale bikes from the Woodside church where he worked on weekends, and stayed around after nearly every delivery to make repairs on those bikes. Our landlord's father and his wife, along with some of their neighbors from nearby Butano Canyon, volunteered their trucks to take bikes to Santa Cruz where the husband of the pastor at Santa Cruz UCC church offered to make repairs. And because Santa Cruz is several miles south of Pescadero, our truck-owning volunteers would pick up the repaired bikes when they went to Santa Cruz for their own business and medical appointments. As the work of Puente Ministry grew there were no coincidences—just grace.

News of the arrival of *bicis* (bikes) spread quickly and the men eagerly signed on to a growing list of those who would like to have bikes. When we got bikes, it was like opening a jar of *miel* (honey). Workers swarmed in like bees! The moment we started to unload, there was a constant stream from the *taquería*. While some anxiously waited at our garage door, others sat very much at home on our front porch or stood in the yard. Often these volunteers crowded in to help the church folks offload the trucks and trailers, riding the bikes back to the shed to test them out. We received precise reports about which ones needed adjustments to *las llantas* (tires) or *la estrella* (gears). Some of the men worked on *los frenos* (the brakes) or changed the height of the *sillones* (seats). I overheard the younger workers talking about which one would be their dream *bici* when they were ready to be distributed. There was electricity in the air; it was a little like Christmas morning!

As each man got his bike, we all gathered to bless them on their way. It felt a little like a sacred communion as we, in community, shared these resources, which were once broken and had now been made whole by the loving touch of those willing to serve. It was a time of transformation for all who participated, showing up and sharing. Like in the story of the loaves and fishes, we always had enough. As we parted those evenings, it was with a great sense of God's presence and peace.

The men rode their bikes daily. And because much of the riding was on gravel roadsides, tires blew out often, it became essential that the men learn how to apply a good patch and replace the tire securely on the wheel rim themselves. Fortunately, Ed was willing to come into town after his workday to help the guys learn to do this, and to make some other minor adjustments on chains and brakes. And Rich, the owner of the Half Moon Bay Bike Shop, came to town from time to time to offer *un taller de reparaciones* (a practical repair workshop) that taught the men how to maintain their "wheels."

When we were well into this collecting-and-giving-out-bikes program, we unexpectedly received information from Community Action Agency (CAA) about a bike giveaway they were sponsoring. This organization was created as a result of the Economic Opportunity Act in the '60s by then President Johnson. Its mission was to change people's lives, embody the spirit of hope, improve communities, and make the United States of America a better place in which to live. Imagine it! And what's more, CAA's focus that year happened to be improving transportation. So we joined with the director of the local Farm Bureau to apply for that grant.

CAA awarded us thirty thousand dollars—an unimaginable gift! That was enough funding to buy and distribute up to one hundred new bikes complete with *cascos* (helmets) and repair kits—but the bikes could go only to people who met specific low-income qualifications. We had two months, October and November, to register the qualified workers and to distribute these gifts.

This came at a time when we were in "high work season," so finding a hundred folks who were not currently earning more than the minimum wage required by CAA was not easy. Our laborers were earning $6.75 at the time, *el mínimo* (the minimum wage) in California, but more than the Federal minimum of $5.50. Because they earned "too much," *estos trabajadores no pudieron calificar* (these workers could not qualify). We did find some who met the qualifications—day laborers, people out of work, or newcomers to the region. And we found *esposas* (wives) and *mujeres* (single women) who qualified, too—women who certainly needed transportation to work, especially when their *esposos* (husbands) took the family car. But in the end, we were able to qualify only eighty applicants. And so we bought the eighty bikes, and returned the rest of the money to CAA (a gesture they had never experienced before). We were glad to return the unused portion so that others could benefit. This was one of those special opportunities to share the wealth justly.

Some of the bikes were distributed at a wonderful tamale dinner, *una cena gratis* (a meal without cost) at the church. The people who received bikes and their families sat down to eat and celebrate with representatives from CAA, Mathew, our friendly reporter from the San Mateo newspaper, church members, and Puente volunteers.

The rest of the bikes were distributed on another day. On that occasion, Dee, a local goat farm owner and former immigrant herself, gave out bikes with the assistance of a visiting missionary from *la Iglesia Unido de Cristo* (United

Church of Christ). He had come from Guadalajara, Jalisco, Mexico, and was touring the US visiting UCC churches. Fortunately, he was available to help as I had been asked to officiate at a memorial service and could not be there.

As the weather cooled and the rains of winter began, we knew that the men sleeping outdoors or in their worker barracks were almost certainly unaccustomed to such cold at night. It became obvious that in addition to bikes, they also needed warm *cobijas* (blankets). And so we began to collect blankets to distribute.

The first batch of blankets came from people in our church and from friends in the many churches that had gathered bikes for us. Later I began to hit the sales at discount stores. We built up quite a supply in our shed of those $4 natural-colored acrylic woven blankets. We looked for ones that would not show the dirt and could be easily laundered with any clothes.

As the news got around that we had blankets to give away, both men and women whom I had never seen before walked as much as two hours from the ranches as far away as the San Mateo County line to hesitantly ask for a blanket. That broke my heart! That anyone would want a blanket badly enough to walk two hours was almost more than I could endure. I can still remember Pescadero's cold, damp nights now as I casually reach for my down comforter!

Then, as we continued with the blanket giveaways, I began to notice that some workers were requesting blankets over and over! What was going on? What was happening to all those blankets? Surely they were being requested for the newcomers at camps who had no way to come to town. Was I to become jaded, as many had, serving the poor?

Margaret laughed when I told her about the fifth blanket I had just given to one particular guy. "Well, you've told me in great detail how the *ratones* (mice) are determined to live in your storage shed, haven't you? The places where the workers live are not much better than your shed, right? Why wouldn't they have mice just like you do? Mice love to chew on things like blankets!"

Then I got it. Of course! The mice were eating our blankets. The rough construction of the men's sleeping areas would offer many tiny openings for mice to slip through, and it would be impossible to keep the little critters out. I shared the same qualms with Ellen about sweatshirts we sometimes handed out. Perhaps the mice loved to chew them, too.

And so we also began to offer tarps, plastic snap lid boxes, and vinyl suitcases to the workers to protect their food, blankets and clothing from *mapaches y ratones* (raccoons and rodents).

Talking to Margaret about the large numbers of blankets and sweatshirts we were handing out, I realized that when a person works daily in the mud and rain planting and harvesting, everything including socks, shirts, and sweatshirts gets caked with mud. And bodies get even dirtier! Workers who had housing did have showers, so these men could keep themselves clean; but for the people living in junked cars or sleeping in the woods, it was a different story. Taking all this into account, it was hardly frivolous to request a second or third sweatshirt or jacket!

In the first months of the Puente Ministry, we told everyone we met about the men who had come to work in the fields—and their many needs. We explained that the men needed bikes for transportation—and people donated bikes. We asked for blankets and sleeping bags, and they brought us *cobijas* (blankets) and *bolsas* (sleeping bags). It seemed so amazing that when we actually told people what we needed in our community, there was a *brotando* (overflowing, burgeoning) response. This excessive giving can only come when we ask, as Scripture reminds us: "Ask, and it will be given you; search, and you will find; knock, and the door will be opened for you."[7] I drove around the county with my backseat and the *baul de mi coche* (trunk of my car) loaded with simple gifts—*bicis* (bikes), *cobijas* (blankets), and *frijoles* (beans), gifts that improved the

---

[7] Matthew 7:7

quality of life for the men, and that showed them that others in the community cared about them, despite the language barrier.

How tenderly these men responded! The first Christmas morning that Ellen and I spent in "the flood house," we were awakened by a gentle but persistent knocking at our door. It was a soft knock at first, but as we lay in bed debating whether or not to acknowledge it, it grew bolder! Finally, curiosity overcame my longing to stay in our cocoon, and I padded to the door, still in my robe and pajamas. When I opened the door, I saw a family in a car outside. On the porch stood the husband, smiling shyly and hesitantly, yet hospitably, offering me a plate overflowing with fragrant, just-cooked tamales. I knew his family barely had enough to feed themselves, and yet they had come to share their holiday feast with us. Never had homemade tamales tasted richer, so blessed as these were with the spirit of the givers. Our bridge was beginning to make it possible for blessings to flow in both directions!

Often now people would appear either before or after the service Sundays at church asking for *"La Reverenda* Wendy." Sometimes they had a special need, but often they simply wanted to *presentarme* (introduce me) to their *hijo* (son) or *hija* (daughter) recently arrived after a trip across the border alone with a *coyote* (highly paid guide).

One morning Guadalupe, such a mother, came to me beaming with joy and carrying a toddler while leading a six-year-old by the hand. She told me her *nieta* (granddaughter) and *hijo* (son) had arrived the night before! Both the slightly dazed kids and the glowing mother/grandmother embodied a joy that the rest of us could only imagine.

Could you imagine trusting a total stranger with your precious baby or toddler, not knowing of their progress or safety until they arrived on your doorstep or until you were able to scrimp and save for a ride to Tucson or Los Angeles to retrieve your children? It must have been the ultimate anxiety for a lonely mom or dad, and for Guadalupe now, a great joy—a joy that I was privileged to share.

Creating a way for all of us to be part of "a family of choice" was wonderful, especially since so many of us lived far from the places we think of as home. It led us to become a family of God. I myself was experiencing the same thing, and so I could understand it in a fuller spirit. Although a dangerous border did not separate me, it was a long sixteen-hour drive to my family in Washington and Oregon. The distance between me and my family, and my longing to be with them, were painful for me just as they were for the men.

Ellen and I became "family of choice" for these workers and families in part because other agencies in town operated nine to five and were closed evenings and weekends; we answered our door until nine or ten o'clock at night, seven days a week. We became the "after hours" source of help. Often the men and their families had urgent needs that did not come up during regular office hours, and we were glad to be able to meet some of those needs.

Late one evening, Graciela and Davida, with two toddlers and a baby in tow, showed up at our well-lighted home near the crossroads. Knocking softly, they asked for *pañales* (diapers). Ellen and I invited them in, *saludándolos* (greeting them) and *ofreciéndolos refrescos* (offering them something to drink). When we asked if they had *vivienda o trabajo* (shelter or jobs) yet, they assured us that their *compañeras* (women friends) would take them in for a few days. And so we bade them *buenas noches* (goodnight) with their arms full of diapers and their hearts warmed.

Our home was the first stop in town for weary travelers. The gray Puente house had *una vela eléctrica* (an electric candle) in the window, *siempre prendida* (always lighted), just as my grandmother's house had when we were children. We knew the special joy of being able to serve where and when we were needed. On most days, we had a supply of *cupones* (gift certificates) that could be redeemed for meals or *ropa* (clothes) at *La Pulguita* (thrift shop), along with *comestibles* (groceries) in a bag that could tide visitors over during their first days in

Pescadero. *Arroz y frijoles* (rice and beans) was a great bartering chip for the rent that most could not yet afford.

A new clarity began to grow deep within me. Here, with rice and beans in my hands, I felt *las semillas* (the seeds) of my life's call sprout in my *corazón* (heart). This was what I wanted to be doing all day, every day. The church was preparing to pay me for quarter time, and I found myself willing and eager to serve full time in this call. Although my teaching job was full-time pay for a full-time job, it was no longer where my heart was.

Never before had I felt so certain that God was calling me. These Mexican faces seemed to bring God's presence nearer, leading me to a place where I could finally use my gifts to work for justice. I had longed for this through three decades of professional life.

5

Gathering My Tent Ministries

Whoever joins God's liberation movement
must be content to spend time in the
wilderness, to live in tents
and not know what the morrow brings.

— M. Gandhi (1869-1948)

After a year of teaching, I *renuncié* (resigned) my position at Pescadero High School. I felt intensely that my heart was *brotando* (bursting forth) with plans for the growing Puente Ministry. I was not meant to be in the classroom. Teaching had brought me to Pescadero and enabled me to become *parte de la comunidad* (part of the community), but it was definitely no longer my calling.

The first month after I gave notice was hard for both the students and me as we awaited a replacement teacher, but I felt that I owed the school that much. By the fall of 1998, I had ended my 20 years as a secondary school teacher and had officially become a one-quarter-time pastor/outreach worker.

Los miércoles de noche (Wednesday nights) became the joy of my life. Men my age and younger came together in conversation with me well into those nights. We got to know each other, sharing family stories, life experiences, and laughter. For those hours none of us was alone or lonely!

However, this was still only a one-quarter-time job. It was certainly not going to translate to my half of the *apoyo* (support) for our household. I told Margaret one day that I would need to come up with a "tent" ministry, like the apostle Paul, recalling how he stopped from time to time to support himself by making tents. I did not know how to make a tent, but I did know how to look for other part-time jobs to supplement my *sueldo* (salary). In this way, I could continue Puente Ministry and still contribute my share of our family's *ingreso* (income).

Through the generosity of my partner Ellen, I was free to follow my mission and still have time to seek out other calls to serve. Since we are domestic partners, her benefits provided me with health, dental, and vision insurance. Of course, I talked with Ellen about finding more opportunities to serve, and I also mentioned it to other people. Then one night, Ellen told me about a job she had seen posted. It seemed that an interfaith health group in San Mateo County was looking for a half-time director. This group offered health assessments to parishes and oftentimes assisted with parish nurse programs. It would mean getting to know the leaders in the African-American, Latino, Samoan and Anglo churches and would bring me into contact with resources for healing all over the county. This would join *cuerpo y alma* (body and soul) in healing, not only from a pastoral, but also from a personal perspective.

I applied the next day, and they were glad to have my application. They hired me right away, and soon I was traveling up and down the San Francisco peninsula. Blessed *redes* (networks) opened my eyes and heart to the wider opportunities for care in our region.

While in this role, I met many people I would never have encountered otherwise and created for myself a network of resources that were to prove useful during the next years on the Coast. It was there—at our sponsoring agency, the San Mateo County Perinatal Council—that I met Theresa.

Theresa represented the MORE Family Agency on the Coast. As we talked, I told her that I had two part-time jobs, but was looking for a little more to do. She invited me to work alongside her, translating a few hours a week for monolingual Spanish-speaking parents whose children had birth-related *deshabilidades* (disabilities).

In this role, I helped at the local hospitals. There I met with families who had newborn children with disabilities. It was especially difficult for *los papás* (the fathers) to understand and accept these unexpected illnesses with their babies. These confused men had rarely heard of the disabilities their children were born with, let alone what resources might be available to enhance a child's chances for a more normal life. More often *las madres* (the mothers) would have a clearer sense of their children's needs and responses. When a child was severely impacted and the family could not realistically expect much improvement, the father and mother needed to know how their community would support them through this period of adjustment and treatment. I counseled them on all these issues.

We also assembled packets for doctors to give to families of newborns. And we worked with Logan, a local videographer and parishioner, to create a video featuring local Spanish-speaking families who were receiving support and services at MORE. The video featured parents describing in their own words the services they had received at MORE, and pictures of their children at different stages of their development. This gave us a presentation that new parents found easy to understand and accept.

Also, I was called in to help initiate peer group counseling. All of this happening together on the Coast brought hope to immigrant families, helped to heal the damaged relationships between husbands and wives, and supplied critical professional services to a very underserved and isolated population. In the process, I learned about the resources available from San Francisco to Palo Alto.

Shortly after I began that work, Rev. Wilma, with whom I had studied for two quarters of Clinical Pastoral Education during my hospital chaplaincy training, called me. She asked me to come to the Lucile Packard Children's Hospital as a two-hour-a-week *capellán bilingüe* (bilingual chaplain), focusing on

Spanish-speaking families at that hospital in Palo Alto. This position enriched my personal faith and provided me the opportunity to learn about geographically distinct Spanish dialects. These were such intimate and rich cultural conversations! I tried to brighten the days for many a parent and child in very challenging, life-and-death situations. Sometimes a child would be barely clinging to life—or might have just died.

On my very first evening at that hospital, after I put on my badge and slowed my own 'street' pace by saying *El Padre Nuestro* (the Lord's Prayer), I headed for the pediatric oncology unit. At the exact moment I entered the first room, an eight-year-old Mexican girl, Marisol, was pronounced dead. All of her local *familia* (family) was *presente* (present). They sat with her and *la abrazaban* (held her) throughout the night until *sus parientes de afuera* (her more distant relations) could arrive from throughout California and Mexico. They all needed to hold her as she "slept" *en los brazos* (in their arms). Their grief was all encompassing, and my heart broke along with theirs.

It was all I could do to return to that ward at the Children's Hospital for the next eight months as the memories of that grief haunted me. Children *no deben de morir antes de los padres* (are not 'supposed' to pass on before their parents). I was called to this ward time and time again to face the terrible loss of children. These deaths for families were *inaguantable* (unbearable). However, I knew that God was also in *las lágrimas* (the tears) they shed, and *con ternura* (tenderly) I told them so. I was frequently asked to pray or to write their prayers in the book in the *capellita* (little chapel) on that floor. *Orabamos* (we prayed) for the nursing staff, the medical staff, the child, and the families *noche tras noche* (night after night).

Both of these assignments—being a pastoral presence and accompanying these *mamás y papás* (moms and dads) facing hard, and often frightening, decisions about their precious children's welfare—strengthened my resolve to use my language and cultural understandings in whatever way I could to be available. At the time no other chaplain was fluent in Spanish, and support staff were standing in valiantly as translators. This was something I could do with the language, cultural understanding, and professional training I had. Plus, I was aware that my compassionate God was putting me in this difficult place to act out this grace.

As my hours of service at the Children's Hospital continued, Rev. Wilma and I began to keep track of the needs of these families, and to log the hours I served on the units. It was clear that the need was great for a bilingual chaplain; and with my hours to back her up, Wilma began to tell this story to various faith communities. These caring congregations responded by contributing enough to cover the *sueldo* (salary) for a full-time Latina *capellán* (chaplain). This first-ever chaplain modeled for the hospital administration how to become an institution with more cultural humility and grace. And this was another lesson for me. How one served within the boundaries of such a large and complex institution was beyond my previous experience, either in my teaching career or in pastoral service to a small church. Wilma and I had found a way forward where it seemed there was no way. That idea was to become my heart's theme song, with echoes of Santa Teresa's breviary becoming balm for my wounded heart:

> *Nada te turbe, Nada te espante,*
> *Quien a Dios tiene, nada le falta.*
> *Nada te turbe, nada te espante,*
> *Solo Dios basta!*

> Let nothing trouble you,
> let nothing frighten you,
> Those who have God are
> lacking for nothing.
> Let nothing trouble you,
> let nothing frighten you,
> God alone is enough!

> — Santa Teresa de Avila (1515-1582)

59

These three calls, undertaken concurrently with Puente Ministry, patched together my "career" for about a year—and richly broadened my foundational experiences. However, all of them were time-limited, and before long I found myself winding up work and looking for other opportunities to serve.

As it happened, this was an amazing time of renaissance for services on the South Coast. The South Coast Collaborative representing all of the identified age or interest groups within the community was engaged in discussions about the *necesidades* (needs) of school-aged children, elders, The Men Alone, and youth. *Había mucha atención* (there was much attention given) to the health needs of families and workers, and a recognition that the community needed to be brought together for the *bienestar de todos* (common good).

A new program was started through the school district to serve Spanish-speaking families with children in school. This new agency rented a modular office building adjacent to the school district offices on North Street. It was called North Street Family Services—soon just "North Street"—and Carol led its staff. We all started very small. We each had our niche, and we would gather a little group to serve and raise funds wherever they could be found, casually at first, and then through foundations and partnerships across San Mateo County and the Bay Area.

Through North Street, I was again awakened to the reality that even in our own community the lack of a common language creates *un abismo* (a gulf) between people. Not only were there very few bilingual teachers in the Pescadero schools, but at that time North Street's only counselor—Jill, a former WIC outreach person and local Pescadero resident—was not yet fluent in Spanish. I had met Jill through my Interfaith Health Ministry workshops with the Perinatal Council in San Mateo County, and we had gained great respect for one another's work, mission and skills. At North Street, her assignment was to meet with the Spanish-speaking women and teach parenting skills. Part of this assignment was to familiarize these mothers with children's *niveles de desarrollo* (developmental stages) using videos in Spanish. While visiting mothers, she also brought food and baby supplies to those who needed them, and *libros* (books) for the older children. Sometimes she arranged *vacunas* (immunizations) for the babies and young children, and she generally tried to provide whatever *consejo* (counseling) and resources her organization had *disponible* (available).

One day Jill asked if I would ride along and translate for her. Thus began a long-lasting, warm *amistad* (friendship) between me and this very dedicated woman, and a grand opportunity for me to supplement my income with a part-time translating job. *Me caía muy bien* (It was a "perfect fit"). Our rides together to the ranches and houses on the Coast where her constituents lived showed me clearly what the realities of life were for immigrants in our *sudoeste* (southwest) corner of the county. I definitely would not have been able to see what I saw, to learn what I learned, without this collaboration. I found that the *corazones dolorosos* (aching hearts) of the women and children relocated here echoed the *anhelo* (longing) felt by The Men Alone who were separated from their families in Mexico. Both often spoke of longing "to go home."

There was also another agency in town—South Coast Children's Services, led by a woman named Judy—that had long focused on the needs of children and youth. With our new Puente Ministry serving The Men Alone, this meant there were three separate agencies providing a safety net to the mostly Spanish-speaking people in our *aldea* (village) on the South Coast.

Now I had *balancear* (to balance) two part-time jobs—Puente Ministry and my position as North Street translator. And before long I would take on a third. In the fall I was asked to teach a Spanish class to English speakers in the community. This would round out my Puente Ministry experience with English-speaking, long-time Pescadero residents, while providing still-needed additional income. It seemed easy now to imagine holding many part-time jobs—just as the workers did. I had not had a full-time position since May 1997, and God had provided for our needs. And so for the next decade, we followed the path of justice and reconciliation that helped build a more richly diverse community—and God provided without fail.

When I first mentioned to Margaret my plan to teach Spanish in the community adult school setting, she said, "Well, it's about time! Even living in Belmont, I wish I could speak Spanish! It must be hard for the town's people to make a "bridge" happen when so few speak the language."

I found out that there had been a long-standing agreement with Cañada Community College to offer a community Spanish class in Pescadero. Lisa, one of the South Coast Children's Services interns from the University of California at Santa Cruz, had been teaching this class, and she truly loved watching her students *mejorar* (improve). At this point, she had some students who were becoming quite competent and asking to move into more complex lessons. However, she knew that the true *principiantes* (beginners) still needed *su propia clase* (a class of their own).

When she learned that I might be available to teach the *principiantes* (beginners), she was delighted. And I welcomed the opportunity to continue to engage my teaching gifts and become better acquainted with the English-speakers in our community. My work was growing, and traffic was starting to flow across our "bridge" in both languages.

Over the next few years we had over 150 students total in this beginning Spanish program. These students came from the four towns that make up our school district—Pescadero, La Honda, San Gregorio, and Loma Mar. All of them had *ganas* (a heartfelt desire) to do more than *dar le saludos a alguien* (greet someone), although even that alone quickly made a difference on the streets of Pescadero. Many of these students would eventually become volunteers in the Puente Ministry, and later at the Second Harvest food distribution. Some even became members of our church, growing into our mission of working with the "whole" community, bridging the gap in language and circumstances, reconciling differences wherever we were able. They became confident that all of us are members of God's family; thus, all of us are to be loved.

Using the Spanish they learned in these classes, these local folks were better able to talk to workers, to hire them, and to get to know the men who were here alone. English-speaking parents from the class were better able to talk to the parents of their children's friends when they had sleepovers. Community members could help their friends or lovers translate and become more comfortable in their extended, and sometimes permanent, lives here in the United States.

Later some of *los hermanos* (the brothers) came to the beginner classes as "teach-dents." And several English-speaking students eventually volunteered to assist in the ESL classes. All of us are teachers, and all are students, as Unitarian theologian Parker Palmer pointed out in the Earl Lectures I attended many years ago at Pacific School of Religion.

These class sessions blossomed into meals together at the corner *taquería* (restaurant), its own *apodo* (nickname) being "*Los Amigos* (The Friends)." Here both the men and the townsfolk were able to expand their conversational abilities and grow genuine friendships.

One family from this Spanish class, Vicky and Joan, invited Gonzalo to live in a guest trailer on their property. They gave him a job working weekends and evenings doing animal husbandry. He gratefully accepted their hospitality and the job, which came on top of his full-time nursery work.

When Gonzalo first moved into their trailer, Vicky and Joan called me to translate almost daily. They wanted to be sure he knew what to do at the ranch, not only when they were home but also when they went on vacation and left him in charge. But gradually, the women's Spanish improved, and Gonzalo's understanding of their English grew, until they all found themselves chatting more comfortably, sitting around the campfire under the stars in the evenings after work. They began to forget the immensity of their former language barriers.

As this arrangement continued over the next months, these two trusting women began to encourage Gonzalo to call his family in Mexico on their personal phone without charging him—a wonderful *beneficio* (benefit). Some time later, they even went to Mexico on vacation and included a visit with Gonzalo's family there. They took gifts to his family whom they had never met. He was quick to tell them what to take: chocolate was a big taste treat; and school supplies for his children, and a nice outfit for his wife, would be most appreciated. While the blossoming of this friendship added "bridge work" that I had always prayed would happen in town, it also provided a welcome example of what was possible when people *llegaban a ser poder comunicar* (began to be able to communicate) easily.

Gonzalo's need for more than one job was a grim reminder of the financial distress many of the men were in. I began to understand that taking on more than one job——as Gonzalo was doing—was the only way that many men could pay off the *préstamos* (loans) owed to the *coyotes* (guides across the border). An inability to pay off such a loan was a *vergüenza* (shame) too great to *aguantar* (bear). From time to time, I would hear of a man who would disappear in the middle of the night, totally *abrumado* (undone) by this *débito* (debt). One such man did not return to town even when we contacted him to tell him that his teenaged nephew had suddenly died. After that, we were never again sure of his location. Talk about *soledad* (loneliness)!

With more townspeople speaking a little Spanish, and some of the men trying out a little English, there certainly was more friendly conversation and less tension on the streets. But breaking down the language barrier was not the whole story.

Among the English-speakers in town there were few, if any, who had not completed high school. Certainly a good number of them had gone on to college and graduate schools somewhere. I slowly became aware that more than a handful of the people I met at church had advanced degrees, which they rarely mentioned; and, of course, there were all the other retired pastors in our preaching rotation who were seminary-trained. We English-speaking townsfolk were a highly literate bunch.

In contrast, the men I met on the street had very limited school experience—perhaps one or two years of basic education. I rarely found one who had completed high school. The few exceptions were those young men who had lived near Mexico City or another large city. These men often took to English quite easily and seemed to blend into the English-speaking community with some style and grace, garnering jobs that others were not able to manage.

The lack of educational opportunities was a consistent pattern in rural communities throughout Mexico. The majority of men coming from Mexico to work in this country do not have a high school education. Many are able to read only a little Spanish—and would generally be considered "illiterate" even in their own country.

Describing this reality to Margaret, I told her—with my heart breaking—about the plight of a young man named Pedro. Late one evening after work, I stopped by the barracks called *el hospital* (the hospital) for a visit with the men who lived there. I had brought a few sheets of *papel* (paper) and some *sobres* (envelopes) with me, and I had offered to help anyone who wanted *escribir* (to write) a letter home. I remember that the porch light shone mosquito-repellant-yellow on the paper and envelopes I had in my hand. Pedro told me that he wanted to write a letter to his mother, but when I held out the paper, he looked into my eyes and said, "*No puedo hacerlo* (I can't do it)."

At that moment, I felt as if I were called to be the hands of Jesus. As he softly and hesitantly dictated to me, and as *los compañeros* (his buddies) and *los forasteros* (strangers) passed by on their way to dinner, I wrote the words and sentiments that would reconnect Pedro to his *familia* (family). We worked together like this for some moments until finally he was finished. He had said what he needed to say.

Then came the most poignant moment for me. I asked him if he wanted to put his family's name and *dirrecion* (address) on the envelope so they would recognize *su escritura* (his writing). He looked at me with such earnestness, and said, "*¿Dónde* (where)?" I realized that he had absolutely *ninguna idea* (no idea) how to address an envelope! I pointed out the spot on the lower right for *la dirección* (the address), another on the upper left for the return address, and the place on the upper right for *la estampilla* (the stamp). When I told him I would put the letter *en el buzón del correo* (in the mailbox at the post office), he asked, "*¿Cómo es possible que llegue a mi casa* (how is it possible that it will get to my home)?" I assured him that the people in the Pescadero post office would know by *el código del correo* (the zip code) where to send the letter. This was a pleasant surprise to him.

What a gift it was to make such a letter happen, and to show Pedro a way to communicate so much less expensively and so much more easily than monthly calls on *una tarjeta* (a phone card). I could not imagine anyone who did not know how to write or address a letter! But this was *un estilo de vivir* (a way of life) that Pedro taught me. I was gifted with a new understanding, and I swore I would never again assume I knew what someone else knew. The student was ready, and the teacher had appeared!

As connections grew between English- and Spanish-speakers in town, we all benefited. English speakers who were strangers to one another began to offer each other rides to Spanish class. Spanish speakers began to share meals and study time. And because everyone realized the dangers of walking and bike riding in the dark, bikes were often tossed into pickups and station wagons after class, and workers were escorted home. Before long there was a general effort made to be sure we all arrived home safely.

This commitment to learn Spanish on the part of many in the community contributed tremendously to the Puente Ministry. From that class grew a cadre of verbally-able volunteers who strengthened the "bridge" between the two language families by offering the men free trips to the airport, to a doctor's appointment, or to the laundromat in Half Moon Bay.

Friends offering rides to friends sounds like a singularly positive development, but it had some unintended consequences. The rides cut into the business of at least one local person, Bill, who had made a *negocio* (business) of providing rides to laborers who wanted to go to the "other side of the hill" or to the *aeropuerto* (airport). Rides with Bill were *muy caro* (costly), and the workers did not have a sense of *confianza* (trust) in him because Bill was a stranger. In addition, some of the workers who had vehicles themselves earned a little money providing rides for other men they knew, and *they* were certainly not strangers. The net result: some in the community really benefited while others lost out. Although we were trying to build a "beloved community" where the needs of all are met, we could not meet the needs of everyone all the time.

To my great *gozo* (joy), I began to hear people asking after a man when he was absent from an event. Noticing one another's absence seemed the right and just thing to be doing—and we all came to know that others were waiting for us. I told Margaret that this reminded me of the parable of the "The Lost Sheep." When we are all together, content in our own circle, and one person—or sheep—has gone missing, it is our call to go out and find that individual. Not only must we find the missing, but when any are out of community, out of relationship, unheard, looked at askance, misunderstood or ignored, we must bring them quickly back into the fold.

My days were now wonderfully *llena* (full), riding along with North Street's counselor on trips to the ranches, meeting with my Spanish classes, and continuing *encuentros* (encounters) with the workers. I often found myself driving here and there, backseat piled high with blankets, sweatshirts, and food. One Sunday a congregant named Detlef stopped me as I was leaving church. "Would you like *una camioneta* (a station wagon) to use for Puente?" he asked.

A vehicle! That would be a blessing—and quite convenient. I told him, "*Te lo agradecería* (I would truly appreciate that)," and we agreed to get together and see what it would take to make that happen.

When I discussed that idea with Margaret, she questioned the *detalles prácticos* (practical details), as she often did when we met. She reminded me that we would need to figure out how to deal with *el título, manejadores autorizados, mantenimiento, y la aseguranza* (ownership, authorized drivers, maintenance, and insurance issues) on our tiny *presupuesto* (budget). Later, when I actually drove the station wagon and talked again with its owner, we decided that the cost of putting this vehicle in good running shape made it unsuitable for the Ministry. But now I had the idea that a Puente vehicle would be a great asset to facilitate the delivery of our services around the region.

I discovered that the church carried an insurance policy that would accept liability for a vehicle used in a church ministry program, so that took care of the first issue and led me to an understanding of how to handle ownership, too.

It wasn't long before Ray, our long-time citizenship coach, offered a different vehicle, a Plymouth van. This one I accepted. *¡Qué milagroso* (how miraculous)! It would be perfect for carrying both people and supplies. In short order we took care of the paperwork and Puente had its own van! Quickly we ordered up two magnetic signs with our logo, and stuck them on the sides of the vehicle so that Puente Ministry was clearly identifiable as we entered ranches and farms, and toured folks around the area.

Now I was more fully employed, mobile, and getting to know many of the people in my new community. But just being in a place with others doesn't mean that you become friends. After all, people in church just see the back of each other's heads *semana tras semana* (week after week). They really don't get acquainted either. It is in the coffee hours, pancake breakfasts, meals, crises, celebrations, prayers, singing, and work projects that the church family comes together. For me it was during informal times—the everyday visits on the streets and at the ranches—that I got to know people. Going where the need is, I became a regular visitor to the *desconocidos afuera del pueblo* (strangers outside of town). I knew that my smile, my practice of making direct eye contact (which was at first suspect to newcomers in town), and my warm handshake invited people into real conversations with me. I was learning not to make any assumptions, and to take plenty of time to clarify my questions or the details of a conversation. It was not really different from getting to know anyone, anywhere. However, with The Men

Alone, I did try to add an extra filter of cultural sensitivity. Quickly they found out that I treated their conversations with *cuidado* (care) and that I maintained *confianza* (confidentiality). The men felt that I could be trusted to hold their stories with *ternura* (tenderness).

And it was in the casual talks with The Men Alone, our brothers, that I began to understand their *razones* (reasons) for coming to the US and their *ganas para regresar a Mexico* (burning desires to go home), to be *reunido* (reunited) with family and friends. Home is the place where *los oleres, sabores, vistas, sentidos y los sonidos nos llenan* (smells, tastes, sights, feelings, and sounds fill us) with what *los almas anhelaban por fin* (our souls longed for at last). With this in mind, I started to talk with church members and volunteers about the possibility of offering "Puente meals." I imagined that these would be *cenas familiares* (family meals) in the home of a townsperson to which three or four men might be invited.

It wasn't long before Linda and John volunteered to host such a meal. They had recently come to the Coast and were particularly interested in widening their own multicultural experience because of their adopted daughter Nora. And so, one evening, I used the Puente van to shuttle Gabriel, Tato, Tino, and Edilberto to John and Linda's home in La Honda. Of course, the men were *bien vestido* (very dressed up) in *sombreros, botas y cinturones de cuero, camisas bordados y joyas* (classic cowboy hats, leather-tooled boots and belts, and embroidered and bejeweled shirts). When we first arrived, we all played outdoors with Nora and a *cachorrito* (puppy). Nora had been bouncing on their gigantic trampoline, and it wasn't long before the brothers gathered up their courage and give the trampoline a try, too. They had never *brincado* (bounced) like that before. It was wild! Later they enjoyed an Italian meal complete with *postre* (desserts). These men were stunned to be in a private home after years in barracks and barns, and deeply touched at being invited *en toda confianza como si fueron familia* (and trusted as if they were family).

Sweet comments came to me on the ride home in the van, bursting forth: *"Qué comimos* (what did we just eat)?" *"Sabroso, ¿pero qué fue* (tasty, but what was it)?" On another evening, Wendy, *mi tocaya* (one with the same name), invited several neighbors and a car load of men for dinner and prepared a Mexican meal. On the way home those men had lots of comments. *"¿Porqué nos preparan comida mexicana? Es lo que comemos todos los días* (Why do people want to fix us Mexican food? We eat that every day)." Or, *"¿Híjole, cómo fue que ella podía cocinar una comida mexicana tan deliciosa? Y por si acaso, está casada* (Wow, how did she know how to make such a great Mexican meal? And by the way, is she married)?"

There were more of these joint meals over the years, and each time the men gained a tiny *descanso* (respite) from days of *soledad y echando de menos* (loneliness and longing for) their families, *fiestas* (parties), and all the national holy days. These brothers' *gratitud* (gratitude) was always effusive. It was as if they had been invited by the President of the United States, or royalty. And their hosts reveled in their appreciation.

But *sonrisas y risas* (smiles and laughter) did not happen every day. There were also *frío, triste, miedoso* (cold, sad and scary) times. One day Baudelio, frightened and frantic, happened to run into me by the post office just after he had gotten the news that his son Antonio had been taken off to *carcel* (jail).

Although many of the single men and families from Mexico were not practicing *católicos* (Catholics), they remembered the Catholic Church from their home villages as being a source of *ayuda y esperanza* (help and hope). Pescadero did have a Catholic mission church, St. Anthony's, and during my first couple of years in Pescadero, the church still had a priest who lived in town, Father Medina. Unfortunately, he was yoked to three parishes—Pescadero, La Honda, and Half Moon Bay. His home was the clothes closet, the transportation center, and the confessional. This gentle man was as welcoming as any faith leader in our community could be. But soon after Puente's beginning, Fr. Medina was transferred to San Francisco. As a result, from then on traveling *padres* (priests) would come to Pescadero on a rotating schedule to say the Saturday night Spanish Mass. Often a different priest said the Sunday morning English mass. The Catholic community had no daily, local, on-going spiritual support. It was during this period that Baudelio met me in his panic.

Baudelio's son Antonio had been riding in a car with another young man who was driving *sin licencia* (without a license). They *chocaron con* (crashed into) another car, killing *la chofera* (the woman driver). Antonio and the driver panicked, jumped out of the car, and ran, but were caught later in the hills by the police. Of course, they were both taken into custody.

Together Baudelio and I got on the phone, calling our local law enforcement officers. They referred us to the county jail, and then to another agency, and after many hours of inquiries, we found out that the authorities had decided to transfer Antonio to a low-risk detention center in La Honda near his home.

When Antonio was released, he was shaken and grateful to have had the contact and the grace of those who believed in him. Stereotypes and fear of the stranger was becoming a thing of the past by now in Pescadero. The faith community had taken in our brothers and sisters to live in *bondad* (kindness) with them, and the townsfolk had begun to realize that we are all in this together...just as the ranchers and farmers know we are connected by weather, soil and crops. This is our community.

And now, each time anyone drives by *el faro* (the lighthouse) at Pigeon Point and sees the cross and flowers, a *memento* (reminder) of the accident, we pray for the woman who lost her life, and also for Antonio and his family.

Another car *choque* (crash) that year on the Coast Highway took the lives of a young mother, Maura, and father, Roberto, who were *hermano y cuñada* (brother and sister-in-law) to one of our men, Arturo. Their toddler Celia *sobrevivió* (survived) the crash, but *la dejó sola* (she was left alone). My friend Jill at North Street Family Resource Center searched for a relative who might serve as guardian. Celia's *tía fue descubierta* (aunt was found) in nearby Santa Cruz, and she was willing to take Celia, bringing a hopeful resolution to the *tragedia* (tragedy). Soon after, they moved to Santa María, and we lost contact. How much worse this might have been if we had not known it was ours to take care of the widows and orphans. Clear messages from our God showed us the path.

Many of our brothers who did drive cars drove very slowly to the laundromat in Half Moon Bay—the closest laundromat available *con agua caliente* (with hot water). A few would speed, not even drinking, but whether they drove fast or slow, some were ticketed. They would spend days in *corte* (court) under the care of a Puente volunteer and court-appointed *traductor* (translator) who valiantly tried to help them thread their way through the system.

One day Primitivo appeared with a ticket in hand: it was for no license, no title, no insurance and an actual minor infraction of driving too slowly and obstructing traffic in the city. Primitivo *tendría que pedir tiempo* (would have to ask for time off) from his job to appear in court! Jaime, a long-time Puente volunteer, met with Primitivo's boss to explain and confirm that he would need to have release time to go to court. His boss agreed to let him go, but the time would be unpaid. Primitivo asked me to mediate, and so we went to court together. We were told we would have to come back to that courtroom a second time after he had gone to "Mexican Driving School"—a three-hour evening class that cost $100. How did he get to Driving School, you might ask? None of his friends could drive legally either. Somehow in the dark of night, he made his way over the hill to Redwood City, passed the class, and picked up his *certificado* (certificate). *¿Esto fue un milagro? No, pero así es.* (Was this a miracle? No, but that is what happens.)

We made the next trip to court for his final *fecha* (date) carrying the certificate and $1,283 to cover the fine. As it was his first offense, the amount was reduced. We paid and returned to Pescadero after a quick stop, at his insistence, to buy us hamburgers, fries and shakes.

Some of our brothers in similar situations had their cars impounded and never did retrieve them: they could not pay the fee and did not have the proper papers, license, or insurance. Driving proved to be a costly proposition for these men, and most stuck to bicycling or walking.

Working through these sad times, I was reminded yet again of *el privilegio de los Anglos* ("white privilege"), of having a voice and no hesitancy in speaking up! Individuals within the Spanish-speaking community were truly *sin voz* (without a voice) in these times of tragedy. They had no legal status here, no money or transportation, and no way *para mejorarlo* (to make it better). Acting as an ombudsperson became an important role for me because I could collaborate with the authorities. I had a *voz, transporte, experiencia y aceso al dinero* (a voice, transportation, experience, and access to money). I would intercede whenever it was necessary, in as many ways as I knew, in order to bring about a just, compassionate outcome. In this way, too, I was helping to build bridges through service.

As we grew to trust each other, we came to recognize that both Spanish- and English-speaking people have the same tender love of family, need for work, and hope for a future that is *seguro y cómodo* (safe and comfortable) for our beloveds. Puente Ministry was breaking through the language barrier, improving the transportation possibilities for the men, and supplying blankets and sweatshirts to keep the men warm.

¿Pero todavía no tenían hambre (but weren't they still hungry)?

6

Feeding Body and Soul

Those who are generous are blessed
for they share their bread with the poor.

— Proverbs 22:9

During the winter of 2001, the men hunkered down like bears in hibernation. Had it been a normal year, before the tragic events on September 11, many men would have gone home to Mexico when the crops were harvested. They would have stayed with their families through the winter, celebrating the holidays and catching up with their friends. Then in the spring, they would have returned in time to prepare the fields for planting.

But in 2001, they did not go home. The trip south would have been no problem, but returning across the border had become another matter. And unfortunately, *no había trabajo* (there was no field work) in Pescadero during the winter's rainy season. From November to May, only the men employed in *las vidrinas* (the greenhouses) had continuous work to do—and it was often part-time. This meant that all the rest were idle, picking up the odd job now and then. It was not hard to see that many were simply without work and therefore without *sueldo* (income). The fallout was that they were here, still paying rent, and left with very little, if any, money to spend on food. I watched as my new friends struggled to keep their stomachs full.

Finding and cooking healthy, nutritious food was always a problem for the workers, but during the slack season it became much harder. At best they might prepare a typical burrito which would contain *arroz, cebolla, papa, y a lo mejor algunos pedacitos de pollo, carnitas, o res* (rice, onion, potato, at best perhaps some bits of chicken, pork, or beef). Living as some did with minimal kitchen amenities, their choices were limited. Occasionally I would talk with a man who had a small *jardín* (garden) around the back of a garage or in a flower bed beside his house or at a *casa del vecino* (neighbor's home). One thing for sure, there was not much milk or many fresh vegetables—not much calcium, vitamins or iron—in their diets while they worked here in the States. Now they were stuck here year-round which further hampered their *aceso* (access) to food and ultimately impacted their *salud* (health).

One chilly fall day as we lingered over salads, I shared with Margaret the stories some men told me of those harrowing border crossings, and the decision on the part of most of the workers to simply remain in Pescadero this winter without work. She looked puzzled and asked, "But I thought they were "immigrants." Why would they care about returning to Mexico? I don't get it."

I tried to explain that these men were really not immigrants in the usual sense. Certainly not in the sense that we had read about long ago in our American history classes! The single men who came to work in *los files* (the fields) usually did not intend to stay very long. In fact, in Pescadero there were no true "migrant workers" who would leave to follow crops. We were an agricultural community, with a group of able-bodied Mexican workers on almost every farm and ranch.

I told Margaret how the men left their wives and children very reluctantly, *desesperados* (desperate) to work here for a few months and send most of their wages home. They *esperaba* (expected) to return to their homes when the growing season was over. About half the men had *sus propias familias* (their own families) in Mexico and the others had *padres, abuelos y novias* (parents, grandparents, and girlfriends) to return to one day.

Their first goal was to pay off the money they had borrowed from their wider families—small loans that they had combined to pay the large sums of money required by the *coyotes* (guides) who took them across the border. Once the travel loan was repaid, many of the men *querían pagar* (wanted to pay) for their children's education. In Mexico, a family *está obligado de pagar* (must pay) tuition, buy *libros* (books), and provide *zapatos* (shoes) for the child who attends a local school, along with fees *para cubrir* (to cover) maintenance of the school. These men who never had the opportunity to get an education themselves *estaban dispuestos a sacrificarse* (were willing to sacrifice) to provide that chance for *sus niños* (their children).

Later, a man might come north to earn money to build a house, or to expand the house he already had, so his wider family could have *un hogar* (a home). And finally, a man might like to earn *bastante* (enough) money to buy a vehicle to drive home in. Most of the men I talked to never intended—or even wanted—to remain in the United States. They were certainly not "immigrants" in the usual sense; they were more like indentured servants who worked to pay off border crossing debts and provide life support for their families. "Home" was some place in Mexico. Their hearts remained there, and their hope was to return quickly to their loved ones. *La mayoridad* (the majority) of the men I talked with never showed the slightest interest in becoming "Americans"!

During that first *invierno* (winter) of limited travel, I heard many stories of traumatic border crossings. For men who made their first crossing in the late '80s, the cost to arrange *pasaje* (passage) over the border with *un coyote* (a guide) whom they knew had been between $400 and $800. Over the years, that fee had increased as the difficulty of crossing grew, and by 2006 the fee was as much as $4,000 for *cada persona* (each person).

The rise in *precios de los coyotes* (coyotes' costs) was due in part to the fact that the men could no longer use the *coyotes* they knew: many of these people had dropped out of that *negocio peligroso* (dangerous business). This forced a man to find a *coyote* who was a stranger, or one who was involved in drugs and people smuggling. What had been a very simple trip had become an expensive, often dangerous, and always a scary passage.

For a man or woman coming from the southern Mexican states and seeking work on the Pacific Coast, *estas entradas* (these crossings) might begin with a long bus ride from Oaxaca up to U.S. border crossing points in either Arizona or California. For others who wanted work in the Chicago/Midwest region or the East Coast agricultural job market, the crossings were through *las fronteras* (the borders) of New Mexico and Texas.

To cross the US/Mexico border, some people faced a day, or even several days, of walking in the high *desierto* (desert), while others crashed through the crowded highway check stations at Tijuana or Calexico, hoping not to get *agarrado* (caught)! A few men told of being concealed in the extra gas tank of a truck, or beneath the false floor of a van, and slipping in undetected that way.

One man told of a *grua* (tow truck driver) who invited him to ride across the border while wearing the uniform—complete with name patches—of the towing company—and thus "passing," literally and figuratively. *¡Qué riesgo* (what a chance to take)!

I had assumed that *coyotes* were all men, but the brothers and sisters told me of women who took people over the border, too. And there were always a few women alone who made the difficult journey themselves. Guadalupe was one of those women. She became part of the first group who met on the church steps for Bible study. Later she came to show me her blessed *hijos* (kids), who had come to join her, brought across the border alone by a female *coyote*.

"I wouldn't mind paying those amounts of money if I thought it were going to help someone's family," Guadalupe told me, "but I knew the money for my last few crossings went to drug runners—and that made me mad." I heard this over and over.

"They even stole our money and left us to find our own way," Martín told me. He went on to describe how he had found *coyotes* that would provide *pasaje seguro* (safe passage) by talking with others, and he depended on re-contacting these *coyotes* whenever he made the trip. But not everyone *tenía mucha suerte* (had such luck).

Gerardo and Felix told of being held in old houses somewhere in San Diego or L.A. after crossing the border until the rest of the money required for passage could be wired to the *coyote*. These "holding tanks" had little more to offer than water to drink. It is rumored that a guard with an AK-47 stood watch over the *prisioneros* (detainees). Since their freedom was contingent upon finding the balance of the crossing fees, many had to borrow heavily from family and friends *aquí en los estados unidos* (on the U.S. side). No one in Mexico had that kind of money to loan.

Others told me of the *escorpiones* y *culebras* (scorpions and snakes) they encountered, and of the cuts and bruises they endured from cactus *espinas* (spines) as they hiked blindly across the alien Sonoran and Arizona deserts during those starlit nights. Sometimes, they claimed that fellow walkers stumbled and died during those nights—and their guides did not even notice. *No les conocían ni de nombre* (they did not even know their names).

While they walked in the Arizona desert, some said they saw *banderas azules* (blue flags) waving on tall wands, marking the water barrels left by some compassionate souls. This project sounded familiar, and so I checked the Internet. *Fronteras Compasivas* (Humane Borders) is an ecumenical group of volunteers who assist in safe passage through the desert. It is staffed by countless volunteers, many from the Disciples of Christ and the United Church of Christ in Arizona. According to their website, a specific number of water tanks with these blue flags could be legally set up on tribal land of the Tohono

O'odham Reservation. With these in place, water was available and the travelers were somewhat less visible to the Border Patrol and Minutemen.

To their credit, the Border Patrol does pick up would-be workers who need medical attention during their crossing and take them to medical stations, probably saving some lives. But after attending to their immediate physical needs, the Border Patrol escorts them back across the border.

One year, several of us from Puente Ministry—one of our advisory board members, Jill; our seminary intern, Billie; Ellen and I—took a retreat trip to work for a few days with *Fronteras Compasivas* (Humane Borders) on both sides of the border. We went as part of a Western Hispanic Ministries Strategies Team, and El Bien Pastor Congregation hosted twenty-five of us at their annual gathering. Over those few days, we shared in worship, dance, and educational lectures. We also visited with border patrol agents and saw for ourselves what this desert crossing area was like. Much of our service there required us to repair water spigots on the tanks at the water stations—vandalized by someone who did not appreciate these resources placed for the safety of the immigrant travelers. The water stations were drained constantly, and all we could do was follow the trail and make it right for the next *viajeros* (travelers).

Another task was to clean up the paths. We filled garbage bags with the bits of life left behind—the *mochilas, unos zapatos del niño, botellas de agua vacías, latas de atún, chaquetas,* (backpacks, a child's shoes, empty water bottles, tin cans of tuna, jackets)—all the things that the walkers were too weary to carry any longer. All of us took home indelible memories of those desolate and forbidding paths.

It was no wonder that the men in Pescadero no longer felt safe in returning home during the slack season. One urgent need was to supply them with food and basic necessities. As winter closed in on the community, I faithfully carried twenty-pound bags of rice and beans in the car, always ready to drop them off for any who could use them. Our shoestring budget stretched to cover these purchases. Sometimes I also gave away donated bags of *manzanas y naranjas* (apples and oranges) or *comidas en latas* (pop-top meals in a can).

I looked for foods that these isolated men could convert easily into nourishing meals, regardless of whether they were living in the *selva* (woods), under the *puente* (bridge), in *un carro* (a car)—either broken down or running—or in ranch housing.

Second Harvest Food Bank, serving San Mateo and Santa Clara Counties, distributed food regularly in Half Moon Bay. One morning, a North Street staff person called to ask if I thought we could handle the logistics for a distribution in Pescadero. I agreed that there certainly was a very real need, and so Carol—the executive director of North Street Resource Center—initiated the request to the Second Harvest office to find out what their current rules were.

With the Second Harvest rules in mind, we agreed that we needed to bring two programs to our town. One would be designed to meet the food needs of the families they traditionally served, and the other would be designed to serve the single people who were our primary concern. Puente would enroll all Spanish- and English-speaking persons who qualified in the latter group: The Men Alone, seniors, disabled elders and adults without children. And North Street would enroll the one-hundred-plus families with children. They had a pretty good idea of who to contact from their ongoing relationships at the schools.

Fortunately, when I mentioned in church about hosting a food distribution, several members offered to help with the actual work of dividing the food into boxes for each family or individual. Unlike Second Harvest programs that some had participated in, this new program would be both ongoing and localized in our village—with food deliveries made to the elementary school *cada mes* (each month). I told them that the first delivery would be Thursday of *la semana siguiente* (the following week) at the elementary school's multi-purpose room. The word went out to La Honda, a town twelve miles northwest of Pescadero. Not only did La Honda folks register to receive food, but many also volunteered to drive down the hill to provide extra hands in the process.

The Pescadero program was different from most Second Harvest programs. Family units were generally allotted a given number of pounds of food. In our case, non-family group—adults without children in their household—were able to request items from an extensive menu faxed to me each month. (We had no fax at that time, and so our good neighbors at North Street shared theirs. This impromptu sharing of technical resources was another example of a bridge, this time growing between local service providers, a kind of easy cooperation that was for me a modeling of the UCC motto: *That they may all become one.*)

Second Harvest required a "membership" fee for Puente to join, plus proportional fees for distributions. These costs were voluntarily paid by the Pescadero Community Church Ladies' Guild, in memory of their program with Second Harvest many years ago. The membership also provided food for the children's after-school homework club and the pre-school's snacks. In addition, the following summer Puente also provided food for the children enrolled in the summer school program. The teachers were very grateful for the *jugo, fruta, galletas, queso* (juice, fruit, crackers, cheese), and other nutritious food they could now serve their students.

Second Harvest provided a multi-column list of all the items they might ever have available, and the distributing agency was to respond with notes about the quantities and kinds of food their group would like to receive. This practice ensured that a community whose inhabitants mostly preferred rice and beans did not receive bags of potatoes. The seeds of cultural humility were nourished for us all, including the agencies who served our population.

The first day I sat down to place an "order," I grabbed a pencil and began working my way through the sheet. We were able to ask for a wide variety of items, including *aceite, pan, pollos conhelados y pavos, cereal, queso, jugo, salmón en latas y atún,* (cooking oil, fresh bread, frozen chickens and turkeys, breakfast cereal, cheese, juice, canned salmon and tuna) along with a variety of canned and fresh *frutas y verduras* (fruits and vegetables). There was a place to order Ensure and toilet paper—and one time the menu even offered *helado* (ice cream)! Finally, after making my best guesses, I deemed it "done" and *lo mandé* (faxed it off).

When delivery day came, our volunteers arrived with eager grins. Not one of us *tuvimos ninguna idea* (had any idea) what we were getting into! Several of the *trabajadores* (laborers) came, too. Clearly, these men were no strangers to work and gave their time to serve others. Here was another opportunity *compartir* (to share) an endeavor and *praticar* (to practice) conversation. Maybe *nos conoceríamos más* (we would get acquainted a bit more).

The truck arrived in the early afternoon, and pallets, *cartones y barriles* (cases and barrels) were quickly unloaded by the volunteers into stacks on the floor of *la escuela elementaría* (the elementary school). The east end of the multipurpose room was designated for the family program, and the west end was set aside for the program that covered single workers, disabled elders, and senior citizens.

Armed with our enrollment lists, we dove into the sorting and were easily done when the first recipients arrived after work. The next couple of hours—from about four to six p.m.—were a flurry of activity with families picking up kids after school, and men arriving from work, all packing off substantial *cartones y bolsas de comestibles* (boxes and bags of groceries), a good foundation for their next month's meals. Kerry—a faithful volunteer, local professional, and neighbor—and Gabriel—one of my closest connections in the worker community—delivered food to housebound elders and the disabled, along with several high school community service volunteers.

After everyone had come and gone, we looked around. There was still food! These *promesas* (promises) from our all-inclusive, compassionate and unconditionally loving God kept coming true! We had been gifted beyond our wildest dreams.

We knew that there were families and single men who had not enrolled—some because they were not yet working and, therefore, had no *talones* (pay stubs) to prove that they were "low income"; and others because they had no transportation to get to the school. Definitely, *las sobras* (the leftover food) could be used.

I was not all that interested in creating paper trails, but of course I faithfully did just that because I wanted to be sure that no one was left out. It was always very clear to me, as God would have it, that a hungry person needed to be fed. These *sobras* (leftovers) were the gifts of God for the people of God— once the requirements of the agency were met. When I was teaching, I was led by the spirit within me to teach *children*, not simply to teach the curriculum. Again, here my concern was feeding *the hungry,* not just to comply with the rules. Wherever one is left hungry, we are all left hungry.

When the registered families and individuals had taken away their boxes of food, every scrap of undistributed food was packed up in clean plastic grocery bags. These bags were quickly filled and loaded into my car. Surveying the piles I was reminded, quite literally, of the story of Jesus' feeding of the five thousand. As I started my van and was ready to take off delivering, *nuestro hermano* (our brother) Gabriel tapped on my window. He insisted that I not go alone so late, in the dark, and with such a heavy load. So unaccustomed was I to receiving help or having someone to look out for me, I felt myself blush in the darkness. He never failed to astound me with his helpfulness, cordiality and gentlemanly ways. Together *los dos* (the two) of us headed up the highway, stopping at *cada vivienda* (every housing unit), even going out to remote ranches, until we had distributed the last bag. It was late! I was really exhausted, and that night everyone was fed.

The Puente van became a familiar sight at many of the ranches in the area as we delivered Second Harvest food bags, rice and beans, blankets and jackets day and night no matter the weather. Francisco, an elderly gentleman, would hang out of the second story window of the ranch near the Costanoa Resort 10 miles south of town calling out "*¡Doña Wendy nos va a visitar!* (Wendy is coming to visit us!)" The bridge we had been building was up, extending south on the coast, and was even more accessible in the years that followed.

Sometimes, no matter how we might try to make sure the men had enough to eat, something went wrong—as it did with Marcelino. This young man, not yet twenty years old, had early onset diabetes, and his usual diet of greasy, fried stuff, sodas and candy would sometimes send him into a coma. When this occurred, it looked frightening. Once his roommates panicked and called 911. The paramedics packed him up and drove with sirens wailing to the county hospital, forty-five minutes over the hill. Swift medical intervention pulled him back from the brink, and in a few hours he was released with directions about what to eat—and what not eat. Unfortunately, the person who explained those meal plans knew little Spanish, and he did not "hear" them. He preferred his current lifestyle— eating the foods he liked, driving his "hog" car—that Grand Am with an eagle on the hood—and chatting with his girlfriend in Mexico on his cell!

The next time I saw his brother on the street, I asked him how Marcelino was feeling. He grinned. "*Ya se fue, mi hermano* (My brother? He's gone home.)" And he went on to say that once Marcelino was home, he'd be okay. Twice this young man had passed out in a diabetic coma and twice he had won a reprieve. Maybe going home *would* be the answer. But we never heard about him again, and I do wonder. Letting go is the hardest part of ministry or teaching. We can ultimately take care only of ourselves.

Puente Ministry was now addressing some of the physical hunger the men endured. Through the Second Harvest program we could ensure that these men had some supplemental food during the long, wet months of *invierno* (winter) and even beyond, as there were other periods when work was scarce. But what could we do to fill the *anhelo* (longing) and emptiness left by their absent families? What could replace all the festive occasions that they were missing out on in Mexico?

As *otoño* (fall) approached and Halloween jack-o'-lanterns began to appear, the community *decidimos celebrar* (decided to celebrate) *El Día de los Muertos* (The Day of the Dead)—one of the most colorful and heartfelt celebrations in Mexico. In one of our first years, before Fr. Medina at St. Anthony's was re-assigned to San Francisco, he invited our church, Puente Ministry, and North Street to join in planning the event. The Day of the Dead falls on November 2, which follows *Todos Santos* (All Saints' Day) on the Protestant calendar. This is a holiday that we all could celebrate because it would fit into nearly everyone's traditions.

I told the people at our church what we were planning, and I made sure that our single men were clearly *invitaron* (invited). On the appointed day, about 125 folks came together at the local cemetery for a service of *oraciones* (prayer) for the dead. Most of the people who gathered for this celebration were our Mexican friends and family whom we had never seen before at our church. *El cementerio* (the cemetery) is a long block from both our church and the Catholic church, so we simply walked together up the road to the hillside's final resting place for locals. We joined in a simple prayer with *velas prendidas* (lighted candles) in hand, and then we *formamos un desfile para regresar a la iglesia* (processed back down to our church). There we shared hot chocolate and traditional *pan dulce* (sweet rolls). The hot chocolate was the Abuelita *marca* (brand) with the *caja amarillo y octagonal con letras en rojo* (yellow octagonal box with red lettering)—a favorite!

Many people offered pictures of their deceased family members and arranged them on the lovely altars, which were decorated with *cempasúchil, azucaritos, esqueletos y calaveras* (marigolds, sugar candy, skeletons and skulls) and indigenous designs and dazzling colors from Mexico. Marigolds are considered the *Flor de Muerto* (Flower of Death) in Mexican culture. All this was an opportunity to share the *belleza* (beauty) and *riquesa* (richness) of that culture. Everyone participated, including some Anglo Pescaderans, *para la primera vez* (for the first time ever). In the following years, the *costumbre de adornar* (custom of decorating) the altar with marigolds, pictures and objects in memory of those who had died was carried on in our church.

Again, a lesson the Anglo community needed to learn was brought to us by the Mexican community through their treasured practices and remembrances, and it helped to fill that ache in our souls—as well as theirs. Let us learn from those we may have held in contempt, seen in harsh stereotypes, considered less than we—and let us offer gratitude for the filling of our souls. All this seemed to resonate with everyone. When we, the students, are willing and ready, teachers will appear.

We were to be blessed with another seasonal celebration as Thanksgiving time came. This was less enticing to the workers than to the church people. In later years, the men did come to enjoy and look forward to this new holiday, but not that first year. Thanksgiving had no parallel holiday in their experience. The brothers received the hospitality of the meal and gathering *sin entender* (without understanding) its purpose, not unlike many of us. We come together and *damos gracias* (give thanks) for the bounty of food and for those who brought it forth from the fields and shared it with us. We eat and *apreciar* (cherish) our *tiempo* (time) with *familia* (family) and *amigos* (friends). Not a holy day, but rather a day of sacred sharing and visible, extravagant offerings of free time, music, and food, including *cajas para llevar* ("to-go" boxes) of *comestibles* (groceries).

Not long after *el día de acción de gracias adornos* (Thanksgiving decorations) were put away, the decorations for Christmas appeared, and although deep inside I might have known better, I turned my holiday attention to December 25.

"But what about *La Virgen de Guadalupe* (the Virgin of Guadalupe)?" one of the men asked. "Aren't we going to celebrate her day first?"

"What's this with the Virgin everywhere?" Margaret remarked, totally puzzled. "Is this something I should Google?"

I relayed a short version of the story of *La Virgen de Guadalupe* that went something like this:

> In Tepeyac, just north of Mexico City, there was a temple for the mother-goddess Tonantzin. It was destroyed in 1519-1521 by the conquering Spaniards. Just ten years after its destruction, on that very spot, a vision of a young woman appeared to a poor, indigenous man named Juan Diego. The young woman identified herself as La Virgen de Guadalupe (Virgin Mary, Mother of God) and asked him to tell the Bishop that she wanted a church to be built in her honor on that spot.
>
> Now Juan Diego was in no position to ask anything of the Bishop, let alone asking to have a church built, but the vision was insistent, and so he went to talk to the Bishop. The Bishop asked for some proof of his experience with this vision. Juan Diego returned to the spot and asked La Virgen for something that he could take with him as proof. She provided a bunch of roses, even though it was winter, and Juan Diego took the roses to the Bishop. Alas, the Bishop was still doubtful and asked for more proof. Juan Diego met La Virgen once more, and this time she imprinted her image on his rough tilma (cloak). He returned to the Bishop, took off his cloak, and revealed the face of La Virgen. The Bishop ordered the church to be built immediately. This story and the spirit of La Virgen somehow binds together the people of Mexico even today.

I also described the *escapulario* (scapular),[8] the devotional necklace worn in honor of *La Virgen* by our Mexican brothers, newcomers and long-timers alike. Having evolved from the

[8] http://en.wikipedia.org/wiki/scapular

large monastic scapular, the devotional scapular typically consists of two small (usually rectangular) pieces of cloth, wood, or laminated paper bearing religious images or text, joined by two bands of cloth. The wearer places one square on the chest, rests one band on each shoulder, and lets the second square drop down the back. In many cases, both the monastic and devotional forms of the scapular come with a set of promises for the faithful who wear them. The faith of our brothers in the saints, in *La Virgen*, and in *Dios* (God) is as much a part of their lives as breathing. It is literally inspiring to be in their presence during these times.

When I asked Gabi, one of our newer friends, about the solace the men found in *La Virgen*, he proudly showed me the sacred image he had hanging from a chain around his neck. It was a gold-framed picture of *La Virgen de Guadalupe* backed in red velvet! Later I saw Gabi actually offer this precious *adorno* (memento) to another man who had recently arrived. "He will need some protection," Gabi confided to me. Again and again, I saw these men who had arrived as strangers to each other becoming *hermanos* (brothers)—and strangers no more. Ever present for each other, bound together by a vibrant faith in the protection of *Guadalupe* and the love of their own women: *madres, esposas, hermanas, tías y abuelitas* (mothers, wives, sisters, aunts and grandmothers). Gabi gave this talisman away, never wondering if it would be returned to him, and maybe expecting that it would be passed on to the next arrival as a token of faith that once one reaches *el norte* (the North), all dreams come true. Who among us could promise it would be so? ¡*Solo Dios basta* (God alone is enough)! And they came, hopeful, sustaining each other with leads on jobs and places to live, confident in the love and protection of *Guadalupe*.

A Belmont Church friend found a good image of *La Virgen*, and I placed her—this tiny *recuerdo* (reminder of "home") —in the Puente office where the men would see her. Similar images found prominence on our altars, in our presentations, and at table. Much later, I counted thirteen separate images around the Puente office. We felt well protected.

In December of that same year, one of the mothers and the counselors from the South Coast Children's Services gathered with Fr. Medina and the high school students to create a *desfile para Las Posadas* (Posadas procession and celebration) before *La Navidad* (Christmas). St. Anthony's celebrated the Posada two weeks before Christmas so that the larger Catholic church in Half Moon Bay could have their celebration on the "right" day, *La Novena* (the ninth day before Christmas).

Our Posada, a one-evening event, portrayed the story of *La Familia Sagrada* (the Holy Family) searching for a place to stay. One student played the part of Mary, another of Joseph, and the younger children served as *los angelitos* (little angels). They walked through town in a traditional reenactment of Joseph's search for hospitality as Mary is ready to give birth to *el niño Jesús* (the baby Jesus). *La canción tradicional* (The traditional song) was sung by the children during this procession is *Para Pedir Posada* (To Ask for Lodging). It begins:

> *En nombre del cielo*
> *Os pido posada*
> *Pues no puede andar*
> *Ya mi esposa amada* …

> In the name of heaven
> I request you grant us shelter
> Given that she cannot walk
> She my beloved wife …

Pescadero townspeople lined the entire path with *farolitos* (paper bags) with beach *arena* (sand) cradling lighted votive candles. At the end of the procession, after *La Familia Sagrada* (the Holy Family) had been rejected at several homes by voices within, singing:

> *Aquí no es mesón*
> *Sigan adelante.*

Pues no puedo abrir
No seas algún tunante...

This is not an inn,
Please continue ahead.
I cannot open
You may be a robber...

We joined together at the "inn" where the Holy Family was, at long last, invited in. The last part of the Posadas song was an exuberant and celebrative retelling of the reception of the Holy Family.

Entren, santos peregrinos, peregrinos,
Reciban este rincón.
No de esta pobre morada
Sino de mi corazón...

Come in, holy pilgrims!
Receive this corner!
Because, even though the place is poor
I offer it to you from my heart!

Cantemos con alegría
Todos al considerar
Que Jesús, José y María
Nos vinieron hoy a honrar!

Let's sing with joy!
Everyone at the thought!
That Jesus, Joseph and Mary
Came today to honor us!

Finally, everyone was happily refreshed with *chocolate y panes dulces* (hot chocolate and sweet rolls). This was another opportunity for us all to celebrate and to share memories of holidays past. It was received with deep gratitude by the entire community on that cold, starry night.

Nearer Christmas we gathered for the lighting of a traditional Christmas tree in Peace Park, with more community singing—this time traditional European carols. Santa arrived on the local fire truck, and the high school youth sold goodies, hot chocolate and coffee. Our communal space was filled with happy voices and colorful, reflective lights in this winter season that had so little warmth, so little work!

The season of these holy days brought the single men, the Mexican families, and the townspeople together in *gozo* (joy), sharing memories and warm fellowship. *El vacio* (the void, emptiness) that the men felt at times was filled through these occasions. We were beginning to address not only *hambre* (physical hunger), but also the hunger for friends and new acquaintances. But we could not mitigate all the *tristeza* (sadness) that *la distancia y separación* (distance and separation from family) brought.

One cold and difficult night, one of The Men Alone brought Porfirio to me. Porfirio was a young man, not long in Pescadero, who was laboring under the delusion that his wife and new baby were somewhere in Pescadero, and he could not find them! He wandered the streets, day and night, calling his wife's name. He told his friends that he caught glimpses of her wandering the streets like *La Llorona*, the mythical weeping woman. His *compañeros* (buddies) called his wife in Mexico so that he could talk to her. She was clearly still at home with the baby. She was living with her parents, *segura* (safe) and *cómoda* (comfortable), and the baby *crecía muy bien* (was doing very well). But this call did little to reassure her young husband.

Porfirio had been forced to seek work up north to support his then-pregnant wife, and he was in Pescadero when the baby arrived. He had only photos *acariciar y abrazar* (to caress and to hold). He was without his new family, and he was *tan joven* (so young)! Soon after his daughter's birth, his *suegro* (father-in-law) called to say that he could not afford the medical costs incurred when the baby was born. Paying that bill required more money than this young man could ever hope to earn—and he still had his *coyote* fee to repay! His terrible loneliness and this newly discovered debt were simply too much to bear. Gabriel and his *compañeros* (friends) tried to keep an eye on Porfirio, but after several days they knew they needed to get help.

The amazing grace in this story is that the day before Porfirio appeared on our doorstep, a *recién llegada* (recently relocated) psychiatrist—a local Anglo—had volunteered her services to Puente. She had moved into a home in Butano Canyon, and our volunteer friends had told her about Puente. This situation called for just the services she had to offer. How timely it was! When we are in need and have nowhere else to turn, we ask prayerfully, or silently listen, and there comes an answer.

I did not want to call 911 and have Porfirio placed on a 72-hour hold at the San Mateo County General Hospital Emergency Psychiatric Unit so many miles away. He would only have been a stranger again, *en otro sitio desconocido y solito* (in another unfamiliar place and alone). And he would have been released on that side of the hill, on his own, maybe *en la media de la noche* (in the middle of the night), scared, disoriented, and far from his farming community home, possibly no better off.

Instead, with this psychiatrist's help, several of us talked quietly with Porfirio and persuaded him to sleep that night in the garage where he was living. In the morning one of the men made sure he met with our sainted, bilingual, county mental health worker, Mary Em. She arranged for medication, and a volunteer took him to *la farmacia* (the pharmacy) to get his prescription. Porfirio and I also shared a private time *rezar* (to pray) at the church sanctuary in gratitude for his care, the care for his wife and baby, and for our ministry and resources. God is indeed good. This brought the brothers who had been watching over him closer as they continued their vigil by night and reminded him to take his medication each day.

This young man gradually found his way back to reality. He met a number of times with Mary Em in the Half Moon Bay clinic, literally carried there by our ever-present volunteer Ray.

The agony of the separation from his wife and baby had been just too much for this young husband *aguantar* (to bear). He was later able to relocate to Texas where he had other relatives, and I hope, by now, he has returned home to his wife and child.

Lesson learned: we are given what is needed at just the right time to serve. It is an honor to find ways to comfort, to make resources available, and to accompany someone at a time such as this.

Another very young man appeared in Pescadero about this same time. He came to find Gabriel, the father he barely remembered. This young man had been working on a cruise ship prior to his arrival in our rural *aldea* (village). Imagine Gabriel's surprise! His son spoke English well and also knew the lifestyle of the rich and famous.

Gabriel and I talked long and hard, looking for ways to make his son understand the value of school and work. But this young man soon left the village, hoping to find a better job than those available here. Being socially bilingual and bicultural, he was used to making good wages. His life was much more akin to those of big city kids—with their street savvy. It was hard on Gabriel (as it is for many families) to see a child lose his Mexican values, traditions, and language.

For both of these young men, our village was not the answer. There were too many differences in expectations and too much separation from the familiar.

Most of the men I knew found *un chispito de solaz* (a bit of solace) in their phone calls home. They depended heavily on the public phones at *Los Amigos* and in front of the post office to stay in touch with family. Even though there was a long *cola* (queue) after work *las tardes* (most afternoons) and on Sunday mornings, the men waited, because these were the prime times to reach their families at the public phones in the town squares of Mexico. (Most families in Mexico had no phone in their own homes.) The enthusiasm of the men when calling home was dampened neither by the distracting street noises, nor the lack of privacy in the side-by-side open booths, nor the unpredictable weather conditions, nor the darkness that settled over them as afternoon turned into evening. In spite of all these drawbacks, the public phone was their *cuerda salvavidas* (lifeline) to home.

When I first came to Pescadero, there were *cinco teléfonos públicos* (five public phones) in town. Over the next few years, the phone company—determining that maintaining all five phones wasn't economically feasible—*quitó* (removed) all but two of them. In spite of this development, I still made sure each Welcome Bag we distributed contained *tarjetas* (calling cards). This way fewer men needed to use *chavitos* (coins) when it was finally their turn to use the remaining two phones. For most of the men, it was *una llamada, la única,* (that one call home, the only call) each month that mattered, that allowed them to stay connected to those they loved. Imagine what *daño* (damage) the loss of those phones did to our brothers!

Geronimo told of calling home one day and hearing his daughter cry "*¡no eres mi papá* (you are not my daddy)!" What a heartbreak for this man who had spent the past *dos años* (two years) providing for his family so they could *sobrevivir* (survive). He later took a job far from Pescadero, riding three hours with people from the church who knew very little Spanish, to help build a home for the Pescadero church choir director and her husband who were relocating. Geronimo was graciously received there and hosted very generously; yet, quietly he suffered much in the winter season. He was well supplied with clothes and heat and food, yet *no fue acostumbrado a nieve* (he was unaccustomed to snow) and wintry weather. When I talked to him on the phone, he sounded *desesperado, sin esperanza* (desperate, without hope) and *deprimido* (depressed), and he *anhelaba regresar* (yearned to return) to the familiar coastside village that had become his home away from home. Everything was bittersweet for these workers, *nuestros hermanos en Cristo* (our brothers in Christ).

Some of the men used their meager wages to buy *celulares* (cell phones). The ads had sounded so good—"Free long distance minutes! Just buy a phone and talk to your family in Mexico for a few cents a minute!"—but most of these phones had poor reception among *las colinas y los valles* (the hills and valleys) of Pescadero. *¡Qué ganga* (such a deal)!

This was not the only cultural miscue that lured workers into spending more of their precious money than they could afford. There were also the solicitations from the Police Fund. In California, we understand that we have the option of not responding to these requests for donations. But in Mexico, if a person were to fail to respond to such a request, he might suffer serious consequences. A police person in uniform usually strikes terror in the heart of a Mexican, whether there is any reason to fear or not. And so, our men faithfully sent support to these public servants whenever a solicitation was made.

While Mexican men work up north, they also miss *las bodas* (the weddings) of sons or daughters, *quinceañeras* (fifteenth birthday blessings and coming out parties), *los nacimientos, los muertes, los primeros pasos y las primeras palabras, los juegos de fútbol, los bicis y los cumpleaños* (births, deaths, first steps and first words, soccer games, bicycles and birthdays), and all that makes family life rich. It is not easy to turn your back on all this, to work long hours in the fields, and to be able to show your love only by sending money orders home.

Indeed, *el correo* (the post office) was the lifeline connecting these men with their families—and also connecting them to those in their local community. Here everyone greeted each other amiably, whether they knew each other or not. The smells of the *los files, la tierra y las cosechas* (the fields, soil, and crops) that flanked downtown were somehow comforting. The bustle of relative strangers holding doors open, helping each other with packages, or petting someone's waiting dog was a welcome bit of local culture we all shared.

For a time the post office was staffed by a Spanish-speaking Anglo woman, and occasionally by a Latina, both of whom made it *bien cómodo* (especially comfortable) for the men to send those money orders to their families. Both these women spoke easily with the men in their own language, and always had lively Spanish music playing in the background. But times do change, and after a while, both women left. The easy spirit that once filled the post office was replaced by a strict adherence to the rules and regulations, and English-only music.

But at least people who had been uncomfortably short of food were now getting more to eat. This was progress. Now I began focusing on the fact that many of the men still had no warm, comfortable place to relax, no place just *to be*—and this became critical as the winter rains began to fall.

7

Finding Our Place—La Sala

Beloved, you do faithfully
whatever you do for friends,
even though they are strangers to you.
Therefore we ought to show hospitality
to such people
so that we may become
co-workers with the truth.

— 3 John 1: 5 and 8

Contrary to the lyrics of the song, rain does fall in California—especially in northern coastal California. Some winter days when the rain pours relentlessly from the sky, I wonder if *esta temporada* (this season) will ever end. We can expect *la lluvia* (the rain) most years from early November through April or May. And during *los meses secos* (the dry months) there is still *neblina* (fog) along the coast, bringing needed moisture from June through November to *las cosechas* (the crops) in the fields.

Before we moved to the Coast, we would notice these changes of season and don our raingear or pick up *un paraguas* (an umbrella), but we never really felt the full impact of the winter's rainy season. However, once we moved to our house on *la tierra de la inundación* (the flood plain), all that changed.

Our landlord had clearly warned us before we moved in that our home was prone to being surrounded by water during flood season. And many folks had shared *sus cuentos de las tormentas* (their "storm stories"), especially stories of the flood of February 1998, which had filled most Pescadero homes with at least a foot of water. But our house had been spared that year, and the owners, taking heart from that reprieve, had lovingly refurbished it to nearly mint condition. It looked quite splendid to us as we moved in that sunny day in December.

Nonetheless, that first January I recall *que estaba cayéndome* (stumbling) out of bed at *llovisnando* (the very first pattering) of rain in the night. As the pattering turned to a pounding, Ellen and I jumped in our "barn boots" and *fuimos de prisa* (hurried) to move our cars to higher ground. Later in the season, we would stuff ourselves into chest waders, just in case.

Those winter storms are notorious for bringing wave after wave of steady, pelting downpour, and for producing copious runoff from the Santa Cruz Mountains. *Las colinas y los files* (the hills and fields) quickly become saturated, and when they can hold no more, the overflow cascades into Pescadero and Butano Creeks in a loud, rushing torrent. Water fills both *canales* (channels) surrounding downtown Pescadero and spills over the town's protective dikes. Then it flows over *la ciénaga* (the marsh), racing and sloshing over the sandbag barriers along the roadway that connects the town with the Coast Highway. That gushing flow inundates the fields and swamps the two main arterial roads into and out of town. Over and over that first winter, we found flood waters lapping at our doorstep.

The gift of a real rain gauge was a comfort. It was provided to us by our friend, Dr. John, who was president of the local church board and long-time resident. He told us that when the rain totaled twenty inches, the ground would be too waterlogged to hold any more water, and we could expect serious flooding. We placed the gauge where we could read it easily, and we found that we knew *cuando esperar una inundación* (when to expect flooding)! For years in our flood house, we were forewarned.

At the first warning of a storm, we would park our cars "up" Pescadero Creek Road, toward the post office, at an elevation maybe two or three feet higher than normal, and in our chest waders, we'd carefully sloshed our way back home. These waders were *un regalo* (a gift), too, from friends up the coast who feared that barn boots might not be enough. We also learned to sandbag around our doors. Our landlord and several of the Mexican workers who lived on Water Lane, where the worker housing flooded even more often than our home, helped us fortify the house with a protective three-foot sandbag wall each year.

We invited our best friend Michael, who is tall and strong, and several other *trabajadores* (workers), to come over to lift our piano and place it on cinder blocks. Everything that had been on the floors had to go *up*, and up it stayed up for the duration.

For most of the flood season, Ellen's regular commute route out Pescadero Creek Road and up Highway One to Half Moon Bay was partly under water. She would drive the Old Stage Road instead, with mudslides or downed eucalyptus trees punctuating that roadway without warning. We would focus on the weather reports, looking hopefully for a break in the storm pattern. Eventually, in what seemed like an eternity but was only a few days, the sun would come out and the waters would recede.

We were spared actual floodwater inside our house each of the three years we lived there, but outside was always a *fangoso* (muddy), silty, sloppy, moldy mess. One Sunday morning in December, Rev. Orril came to pick us up for worship in his old, red, beater pick-up. He arrived with a plank and a heart of gold. With water up to the threshold of our front door and over the back porch, he dropped the plank in a fortuitous place, and we shuttled vestments, guitars and sermon notes into the bed of his truck. We rode like *una carroza del desfile* (a parade float) of royalty to the church at the other end of town. When the water receded, we hosed off the porch, walkways, and grass, and raked the gravel back onto the driveway.

As the fields across the road from our house began to dry out, I saw the men begin afresh to till *la tierra* (the soil). I knew it would soon be followed by planting, then nurturing, and finally harvesting. During that first spring as I watched the fields come to life again, I felt *una connección renovada* (a renewed bond) with the earth, with the brown-corduroy ploughed rows, with new sturdy weeds growing beside seedlings set in place. I had a strange sense of "coming home."

As I later told Margaret, I realized that all this reminded me of scenes from my growing-up years with my own family. I remembered my Uncle Norm and Aunt Mary's cranberry bog in Long Beach, Washington; my Uncle Bob and Aunt Eva's fields of wheat, barley, and potatoes in Tule Lake, California; and my maternal grandfather Pop's garden out back in Longview, Washington, where I grew up. So many memories *me inundaba* (flooded over me)!

In my mind's eye I could also see my dad driving Uncle Bob's truck at harvest time. Earlier in the summers, Mexican laborers taught us kids to siphon water from the irrigation canal into rows of crops. Even though we were little, we still could help. My own and wider family had lived amidst the pivotal seasons of planting, and the cycles of "weather-driven" subsistence, always *surrounded al aire libre tan lindo* (by the beautiful outdoors), aware of how both awesome and awful it could be.

During peak season in Pescadero, it was common for the brothers to report to the fields by seven in the morning, and work there until eight or nine o'clock in the evening. But at other times, the general working conditions, and the expectations of the growers and ranchers in Pescadero, were quite reasonable. In a good season (June through November), a man working full time might clear $1,000 a month. Rent in a few places was free, and when it was not, that man might pay rent from $40 to $200 a month.

But I knew that in their current living conditions, the men *no habían un sitio para hacerse cómodo ni recrearse ni charlar con confianza* (had no place to be comfortable or to relax or chat in confidence). And because they were, for the most part, undocumented workers, they were not in a position to protest or demand anything different concerning housing or working conditions. They were literally *sin voz* ("voice-less"). With the wet days and nights upon us, it was becoming imperative that we find a place indoors where we could gather the men to talk and share stories. Clearly we could not chat on the street corner in the rain for all those months. We needed a "place" to be. We needed *La Sala* (a "community living room").

A year earlier, several of us from church had attended a ten-week workshop on social and economic justice issues at the UCC church in San Carlos. It was offered by the San Francisco Foundation Faiths Initiative on Economic Justice. There we had learned about the Faiths Initiative of the San Francisco Foundation and the Peninsula Community Foundation's Neighborhood Grant Program. And we had learned how to submit a grant application.

That was exactly the opportunity we now needed.

Sarina and I cooked up the whole idea in her *cocina* (kitchen), in a sweet water tower that had been converted into a studio apartment two stories above Pescadero's North Street. Sarina was a recent arrival in town, a woman who from the beginning supported our care of the workers. She also had editorial experience, and so was a natural to join me in writing this grant application. Hour after hour, Sarina and I sat overlooking the *aldea* (village), envisioning ways to make *La Sala* a welcoming place—complete with Mexican hot chocolate, coffee, and good *galletas* (cookies)—and crafting our dreams into a grant application.

And then we were awarded *una donación de una fundación* (the grant)! We knew immediately that we would use the money to rent and staff the Native Sons' Hall. It was *el único sitio* (the only place) in town that could accommodate us. *Este edificio histórico* (this historic building) was built in the 1860s as a

Methodist-Episcopal Church, and reborn in the 1930s as a Japanese Cultural and Language Center. Now the Native Sons and Daughters of the Golden West owned it. The Pescadero community purchased three hundred days of use from the Daughters so that local organizations could rent the site for meetings and other community events.

The hall offered a large meeting room with dark wood wainscoting, *dos baños* (two restrooms), *un calentador* (heater), *luces* (light) and *una cocina* (kitchen). It was more than adequate for thirty to fifty adults to gather, play games, sing, and socialize.

Sarina, also a gifted artist, created our logo, a drawing of *un sofá* (a couch), as a welcoming reminder of the comfort we offered in our new gathering site. The son of one of our head pastors built a sandwich-board sign on which Sarina painted that sofa logo.

As we collected furniture for the living room, Sarina donated her lovely blue couch—the same one that had inspired her logo. That over-stuffed sofa was to become a symbol of a "home away from home," a very real example of living out the familiar phrase *mi casa es su casa* (may my home be your home). God again provided, bringing just the right people together at exactly the right time.

When Puente Ministry first became the "anchor" tenant in the Native Sons' Hall, the building was not in good shape. Over the years it had enjoyed benign neglect. The hissing heater suspended above our heads looked like an eighteen-wheeler's radiator as it provided warmth. Many critters shared the building with us: *ratones, abejas, ratas, y hormigas* (mice, bees, rats, and ants). Still it had an intact roof and space to set up tables and chairs.

During the years that *La Sala* met there, a block grant became available for the renovation of historic buildings, and a grand refurbishing program was carried out by volunteers from the community. The result is the truly impressively *sitio restorado* (restored site) that it is today.

Our original plan was to open *La Sala* two days a week, Thursdays and Sundays. Thursday we would open about five in the afternoon. This was a good time for the men to come in from the fields and have a snack. We would finish up by eight o'clock so they had time both the eat dinner and to fix their lunches for the next day.

Sundays we would start a little earlier. *La Sala* would be staffed by Sarina and Ray, along with occasional townspeople, random visitors, and me. We planned to provide referrals to all the social services available in the area; tables set up for cards and dominos; a computer for internet access, games and language learning; healthy snacks; and friendly people to greet those who came. Once the initial grant monies arrived, we gathered the supplies, and *La Sala* formally opened May 5, 2000.

Ray, who had become *uno de los voluntaries más fieles* (one of our most faithful volunteers), offered to be the regular host. He came in his trusty, vintage pale-green farmer's truck every Thursday and Sunday, and to most of the special meals and holiday events we planned for the men. He soon became the common denominator, the familiar male face of *La Sala*.

He played chess and dominoes with the men, non-verbal games rich with numbers, through which he modeled basic thought processes and problem solving skills. These games became very popular. He also brought *rompecabezas de madera* (wooden puzzles) of the United States and of Mexico for us to put together. These puzzles elicited curiosity, promoted growth in the understanding of *la geografía* (geography), and provoked *preguntas* (questions) from us all about each others' homelands. Here was a way to talk about other places and ways of living with our brothers and sisters—our friends.

Ray's care for the men always extended to knowing each by name and by *el estado de los estados unidos de Mexico* (his home state in the United States of Mexico). He made sure that each man learned to put his name in our sign-in book: Ray would do this for the men once or twice, and then he would gently nudge them into making a signature *como un médico* (like a doctor's), or printing painstakingly. This was another skill that could be transferred to other situations. Although the men could not open a bank account, they were able to sign the money orders that flew out of Pescadero post office or bank *a la quincena* (every two weeks). Ray had helped to make all that possible.

Ray's patience in setting up the tables each Thursday and Sunday, and in making the room into a home for the men, was *precioso* (precious). Others, including Sarina, contributed the technical skills I lacked, helping the men gain some computer literacy so that they could practice their English and search the Internet. Many of the men were delighted to show us their home villages on Mapquest. With some help, they also learned how to scan in and make copies of photos to send home.

Every day, Ray would put out the treats, making sure the *palomitas* (popcorn) was made, and everyone had something to drink, and a place to sit. He even took on the job of recycling all our plastic bottles, and often carried the trash to his own home or to *el dompe* (the town dump). Sarina fixed *el café, el chocolate calientito, o el té* (coffee, hot chocolate and tea) and set out the donated *galletas, naranjas y manzanas, o cacahuete con sal* (cookies, oranges and apples, or salted peanuts). The men would chat, or play the guitar and sing. Sometimes we brought *el piano* (the keyboard) out of the "cubby" of a supply closet where it was kept with all the supplies we needed each day, and someone would pick out a melody by ear.

In between his days at *La Sala*, Ray did far more than anyone ever really knew. He logged hundreds of miles and hours transporting folks to *citas* (appointments) with *los médicos, el dentista, el hospital, la farmacia, o el optomólogo* (doctors, the dentist, the hospital, the pharmacy, or the eye doctor). Those gifts of transportation went unrecorded for many years even in our careful volunteer records.

When we began collecting statistics for grant applications and reports, we were awed by the many volunteers' incredible offerings of time and care. These numbers clearly demonstrated a significant level of community support for our grassroots agency, and this became very important as we began to work to secure more sustainable funding.

Over time, Ray also became a gentle hiring coordinator for dozens of men through his own neighborhood connections and personal recommendations. He even provided rides to some of the men, bringing them to the jobs they'd agreed to do for nearby families.

Of course, during the months of preparation for the opening of *La Sala*, I continued with my other part-time jobs—and I found myself often driving up and down the Coast Highway. It was during these drives that I re-discovered Johnnie Angel, the lone coast walker. Sometimes I encountered him walking north, other times south, and when I could, I would stop for a quick greeting. It was never an extended conversation; we would chat just for a minute or two, but he seemed glad to see me. One afternoon I offered him a jacket and some food that I was carrying in my car for the men. He accepted the jacket, and I felt we'd inched toward becoming friends.

Since our flood house was near the Coast Highway, it was not long before I began offering Johnnie a place *para limpiarse* (to wash up) or *descansarse* (rest) a bit if he needed it, but he always politely assured me that he was fine. He added that he would keep my offer in mind.

As this occasional visiting continued, I began to learn at bit about Johnnie. I learned that he was fluently *bilingüe* (bilingual)—and possibly *trilingüe* (trilingual), since he spoke some Italian, too. We talked easily, going back and forth between English and Spanish, and we found we could talk about almost anything. The man was well-read, well-traveled and quite thoughtful. Clearly he had chosen the life of the road, preferring to be *al aire libre* (out under the sky), always moving on.

When I mentioned Johnnie Angel to Ray, he and his wife, Kay, invited Johnnie to live in the barn on their property. To my amazement, Johnnie accepted and moved in. This generous couple made Johnnie, a complete stranger, comfortable—and he became part of their family.

Ray was indeed one of the "constants" at *La Sala*, but he was not alone. Sarina was the other anchor and supporter. She too came faithfully for years, bringing her home-cooked, healthy treats; the art supplies that the men used to draw and to paint with; and a computer. Her presence spoke volumes about her passion to share our mission.

Once *La Sala* was up and running, we found that— contrary to our imagined scenario of "great coffee and cookies"— *los hermanos* (the brothers) really preferred a jar of Folger's Instant and tangerine-flavored ice cream wafers. Gatorade was also a big hit, along with peanuts in huge family-sized jars, salted, of course. Imagine our surprise! We were absolute willing to offer the brothers what they wanted! How silly we were! We had assumed what might warm our guests' *corazones* (hearts)—without even asking them. Along with a bountiful table, we offered *La Sala* snacks *para llevar* (to take home). This was our way of offering radical hospitality. And we hoped that because of this hospitality, the men would come in out of the rain, find a home away from home, and build their skills.

Almost from the beginning, the men began gracing *La Sala* with beautiful flowers to cheer us. Some of the men who worked on ranches would bring us blooms that had been discarded. *Este ofrenda* (this offering) was appreciated by all of us, especially me. As I enjoyed the colors and fragrance of the blossoms, I recalled singing with the Benedictine sisters in Mexico, "*Brota mi corazó*n (My heart is springing forth) in joy!"

Sarina produced a *libro básico, práctico y bilingüe* (basic book of practical phrases in both English and Spanish), printed copies, and made binders for every man to take home and study. We also found some English-learning *cintas* (cassettes) with accompanying booklets, and we bought *grabadoras* (cassette players) and *audífonos* (earphones) for the men to take home to the ranches. Not everyone had a TV, so this was a great pastime as well as a learning tool. Before long some of the men had built up enough confidence in English to be rewarded with more occasional jobs from townsfolk.

One day we discovered that two of Sarina's students, *Adán y Felix*, had had some schooling in Mexico City before they came north. That afternoon, they had both checked out cassette players and language tapes. Weeks went by, and although they came in for snacks, the only thing they did at *La Sala* was listen to the tapes. After a year of hunkering down with earphones under their *gorritos* (caps)—which were pulled way down so you could not ever see their eyes, they suddenly took off those caps and began speaking nearly fluent English! *Nos sorprendía* (We were stunned) by their new-found language skills! They became our favorite Spanish class tutors and ended up with a surplus of weekend jobs.

New arrivals found a special, warm welcome at *La Sala*. Through my daily talks on the streets with The Men Alone, I knew how much they wanted to be able to clean up and to look "respectable." It was so important to them to recapture some sense of "normalcy" in this totally new place. Usually a newcomer would walk into *La Sala* in the very clothes he had been wearing when he crossed the border and walked through the desert. The trip across the border, most likely, had been *un terror* (a harrowing experience), stripping him of all, or nearly all, his cash and dignity. What's more, he probably had paid an additional $300 to a *pollero* (driver) to bring him *al norte* (north) to Pescadero from Arizona or southern California. A few lucky men had family members who sought them out in Los Angeles or Phoenix, bringing them to loved ones already in *los Estados Unidos* (the United States). But new arrivals in Pescadero were usually alone, ravenous, dirty and exhausted.

Margaret and I talked about putting some bags of essentials together for such men. I wanted to be able to hand each *recién llegado* (new arrival) a "welcome bag" with the basics for washing up, maybe a pair of clean socks, coupons for some hot meals, *arroz y frijoles* (rice and beans), *una tarjeta telefónica* (a phone card) for that important first call home, and our Green Sheet!

When I mentioned the idea to some of the churchwomen, contributions began to appear. One day it was little bars of *jabón* (soap), and another day it was two dozen *peines nuevos* (new combs), *toallas* (hand towels) and *navajas de afeitar* (razors). While I was visiting my sister in Rainier, Oregon, across the Columbia River from where I grew up, we went shopping at a discount store owned by relatives of her husband. The store was advertising "seconds" on tote bags! I bought all they had for a dollar apiece.

As I counted out those dollars to the storeowner, I told our Puente story along with a description of the winter's floods. When I finished, she said, "Don't go! I want to send some things to the kids in your community—the ones who've lost so much with all that rain and flooding." That day she and her husband filled the covered bed of our pick-up truck with school supplies for the children. Pens, pencils, notebooks, backpacks, glitter, glue sticks, paints, paper, rulers, pencil boxes, Pee Chee folders—their gift left nothing out! Again, our world of abundance unexpectedly spun into action!

Wendy, *mi tocaya* (a person who has my same name), one of the churchwomen who lived in the canyon, took the empty tote bags I had bought and the supplies people had donated and began to assemble our first *bolsas de bienvenido* (welcome bags) in her *sótano* (basement). What she didn't have, she arranged to get donated until each bag had a full set of personal hygiene and grooming supplies, and later *cosas para primeros auxilios* (some first aid items). She drove around town with her black Rasta station wagon piled full of bags of soap or socks or whatever she gleaned to distribute wherever necessary.

Fran, another volunteer, shopped for Puente and bought dozens of new *calcetines* (black tube socks), as did Lois, my friend from the Belmont church. Lois haunted the sales and brought bags of socks, along with other items and food, to Margaret, who would pass them along to me. The men asked for black, of course, so that they would look good even after weeks of working in the fields.

About that same time, I was introduced by a community member to the president of Philanthropic Ventures Foundation. He was willing to fund food coupons that could be redeemed for a week's worth of *cenas calientes* (hot meals). The owners and staff of *Los Amigos*, the corner taquería, agreed to honor the coupons at their restaurant and small general store.

New arrivals were often brought to *La Sala* by Gabriel, or Mauricio, or Luz—three "old souls," all of whom I had known since the first days on the steps of the church. Mauricio usually brought *su guitarra* (his guitar), and the men would sing songs they remembered from home. For those hours they were safe, dry, indoors, warm, and among friends—old and new. English-speakers from the church and from Spanish class came, too.

Tourists from the Bay Area, from out-of-state, and sometimes even from Europe dropped in occasionally on Sundays, first peeking in as they checked out this historical building. Some of them began conversations in Spanish; others spoke while we translated. All were "enlightened" by our camaraderie, our mission, and our welcome to them, as strangers no more, too.

Los músicos (the musicians) among the townsfolk brought more music to be played on the computer, keyboard, accordions, banjos, mandolins, harmonicas and guitars. Some volunteers practiced their halting Spanish, welcoming the always sympathetic corrections by the men. Others encouraged the men to try a few words of English—and maybe even convinced a few to take ESL classes.

Ten Mexican men and women, so emboldened, enrolled in a Spanish Leadership Class sponsored by Peninsula Partnerships. Our contact there, Mani, assigned Tato to lead this class and he brought a wealth of wisdom to share with our friends. After the class concluded, these folks, three men and seven women, formed a community group. They had learned how to run meetings, work with the school district, gather data on surveys, listen to the opinions of others, and stand their own ground. This newly formed *grupo* (body) frequently offered *kermes* (fundraiser celebrations) which raised money to pay for childcare training so moms would be qualified to work and earn money. These events also provided money for other elementary school needs. This group became a highly visible "success story."

However, most of the men simply came, played a game, had a snack, and joked with the other guys. Since we could almost count on them eating something at *La Sala*, we made a special point to bring oranges and apples and other fruits. We knew that the men were generally under-nourished and needed to eat more foods rich in vitamins. It was all too easy for them to grab a soda or a candy bar when they were on their own and hungry.

"With all that *azucar* (sugar) they eat, do they ever brush their teeth? I wonder if they have cavities. Can we do something about that?" Margaret asked one day.

My dentist had exactly the same reaction about dental hygiene when I told him, while I was getting my teeth cleaned, about getting to know the single men working on the farms around town. When he finished cleaning my teeth, he pulled open his drawer of "give-away," cellophane-wrapped toothbrushes and sample boxes of toothpaste and scooped up several handfuls, dropping them into a large plastic bag.

"Here, take these. And also these small mouthwash samples. They don't have any alcohol, by the way," he chuckled. "I'll find some more for you when you come back next time." And he did keep us in tooth brushing tools and dental hygiene products, which we passed on to the men. He even gave us a supply to take with us when we went to visit the Benedictine Sisters in Cuernavaca, Mexico.

With a good supply of dental hygiene products in hand, I felt inspired to ask our dental hygienist to come to *La Sala* with a translator and show the men how to brush their teeth and keep their gums healthy. She came several times, lugging a huge cardboard mock-toothbrush and a giant set of teeth. Having two women visit *La Sala* was *un tesoro* (a treasured gift), and the men never took their eyes off of them.

Not long after the hygienist's visit, *Sonrisas* (Smiles) nonprofit Dental Clinic opened in Half Moon Bay. As the men became more comfortable with the idea of taking care of their teeth, several of them actually made check-up appointments. Julia, the Sonrisas executive director, later became a member of the Puente board and helped develop a policies-and-procedures manual with us. This venture into the world of dental health care was a win-win all around. Not only was it an important way to demonstrate our loving care for each of these lonely men, but the contact we made with the Half Moon Bay clinic also blossomed into the relationship between our organization and the wider community.

"Has anyone come back to tell you, 'Look, no cavities'?" Margaret quipped when I told her that some of the men had actually gone to have their teeth cleaned. What a giant step toward taking better care of their health!

That day Margaret and I also talked about the men being for us "the stranger" described in Matthew 25:35-36:

> For I was hungry and you gave me food,
> I was thirsty and you gave me
> something to drink,
> I was a stranger and you welcomed me,
> I was naked and you gave me clothing,
> I was sick and you took care of me,
> I was in prison and you visited me...

"I remember how my mother always fixed a plate of food when someone would knock on our back door," Margaret told me. "Of course, during the Depression, there were lots of folks wandering around in search of jobs."

"My grandma did the same thing for hobos," I replied, remembering my own family's response. "Did you know that 'hobo' is an abbreviated form of 'homeward bound'? In a way, I think of Puente carrying on that tradition."

Now, we could talk about *La Sala,* and know that our "strangers" were being called by name; they were becoming our friends. We were regularly offering physical and spiritual nurture: food, sweatshirts and sox, and fellowship. In addition, from time to time we had arranged care for the sick, provided translations and counsel, interceded on behalf of those in trouble with the law, and provided dental care. Puente Ministry was truly becoming a home away from home for the men. On those rare occasions when the men appeared at a church event, we welcomed them, but we never linked our services to expectations of their church participation.

In return, the men were becoming a contributing part of the *aldea* (village). When floods threatened, they provided willing hands to fill sandbags at the high school for locals to pick up and take home. At *La Sala*, they shared *las verduras* (the vegetables) they grew in their own *jardines* (gardens) and *las flores* (the flowers) they were allowed to glean from the commercial growers where they worked.

One day, Pescadero's Emergency Planning Committee realized we needed a Spanish translation of the Emergency Preparedness Survey used to assess the readiness of our community in case of disaster. We knew it was crucial to reach beyond the confines of the hundred or so homes in the "downtown area" to create a really inclusive disaster plan. We also acknowledged that many of the people we wanted to reach would not be able to understand our questions if they were presented in English.

Fortunately we now knew where to go for help. Our friends, *los hermanos* (the brothers), agreed to come to the La Honda-Pescadero Unified School District offices after a hard workday and helped us translate that survey into Spanish. They also offered many good ideas that improved the survey immensely.

When the Pescadero High School scheduled a renovation project, volunteer workers came from across the nation, and our brothers took part in that work force, too. The same kind of thing happened when the elementary and middle schools updated their playground and garden areas. These men were ready and eager to give back and support the children, no matter whose children they were. On these workdays, they revealed and shared their "real" skills of carpentry, painting, gardening, clearing, and preparing to pour concrete or build stone pathways.

Watching them was quite a revelation. Later we found out that few of them had done fieldwork while living in Mexico. Gratitude runs deep in our brothers who, when they have a place to offer their true skills, are happy to do so. Like all of us, they enjoy being appreciated.

Not only were the men contributing to community projects, but they were also being asked to work on the weekends for people around town. I made up some green business cards on which I could write each employer's name so there was no confusion about who was to work for whom. We had already settled on a particular hourly wage and number of work hours, and whether lunch and/or water would be provided and safety equipment made available. When a townsperson picked up a man, he would be given a card, and there would be no doubt about these critical items. The employer would also know that the man was part of Puente Ministry.

In a few short years, I had moved from casually meeting a few of the men alone on the steps of the church to a fledgling ministry serving fifteen to thirty men a week, providing bikes, warm bedding, jackets, food, grooming supplies and a regular meeting place where workers and townspeople could and did relax together. This was a reflection of the longing that many church people and other townsfolk had had for years—but had been unable to put into action. Its success rested squarely on *el apoyo* (the support) of those same people who provided the *manos y pies* (hands and feet) that assured the activities and services took place.

As we settled into this new routine, meeting with these men regularly in a warm, dry place, Ellen and I began to wish that we, too, could be certain of a warm, dry place during the rainy season. Everyone knew of our winters in the house by the bridge. Often that house had been featured in the *Half Moon Bay Review* or shown on the local evening TV news. When a cameraman wanted to send in live coverage of flooding, our landlord and our little bungalow were shown on the news again and again. No one in town was surprised when we began to ask if someone knew of another place we could rent!

Finally, when our dear friend Michael, a congregant and Puente volunteer, was called to the Southwest to care for his father, he offered us first choice to sublet his house. Our lease on the flood house was up in January. And blessed be! The high school secretary was the daughter of Michael's landlord! Small towns abound in amazing connections—and in this case, it made for good references.

The new place was also on Pescadero Creek Road, but located on slightly higher ground very near *la cruz* (the crossroads). We jumped at the opportunity, packed up our things, and moved ourselves into that gray house only about a half-block from the intersection of Stage and Pescadero Creek Roads: These are the crossroads that include *la gasolina* (the gas station), *la taquería* Los Amigos, Duarte's tavern and restaurant, and *el correo* (the post office).

Now we were settled in the heart of Pescadero—well away from the flood waters. We were free from the anxiety of preparing for or cleaning up after the floods. We were confidently warm and dry. And I was able to focus on my ministry.

Finally, we could hear our own distant families telling us how nervous they had been whenever they heard that another storm was hitting northern California. We also became aware of the level of stress we ourselves had carried through those wet, windy winters. We had shared a version of the uncomfortable situation that many of our brothers also endured. Now we were delighted to be in a more comfortable home, and to know that the men, too, were less stressed and isolated—received, as they were, with grace at *La Sala*.

8

Building Our Foundation

All that we do now must be done together
in a sacred manner and in celebration
for we are the ones we've been waiting for.

— Hopi Nation

uente Ministry was growing fast. Instead of being on-call
ten hours a week, I felt now like I had a full-time job! I
realized that I was depending more and more on
Margaret's administrative help for the functional stuff,
the advisory committee for wise counsel, and the Ladies' Guild
for the unexpected emergencies.

Margaret and I had been talking about my ministry with
the men ever since I made the move to Pescadero, but those
talks began to take on more serious tone when we shifted our
weekly visits to San Mateo—at the salad bar across the street
from her own business. After we ate, we carried our
conversation back to the shop and sat huddled in front of
Margaret's computer screen for hours. There her husband Peter
became our personal "rock" as we began to build a working
organization to support the fledgling Puente Ministry.

Peter served as our onsite IT expert—ready to dash
across the room whenever we yelled help! Sometimes, we
needed help in figuring out how to do something we didn't

quite know how to do. Other times, it was that blue screen, with its awful "fatal error" message. Peter would deftly tap a few keys, and we would magically return to our text or spreadsheet—ready to go. It was during those fumbling, bumbling sessions that Peter's patient explanations and clear descriptions of computer processes enabled me to learn to handle this new environment. I was a pastoral, relationship-oriented person who did not want to get caught up in computer technology, and I cringed in horror when the thing crashed.

As mysterious as computers were to me then, miracles could happen with Peter and Margaret by my side. As it is said, "When the student is ready, the teacher appears." We all have so much to give—and to receive—that will make this world a better place. Truly, no one can do it alone.

Not only did I enlist more of Margaret and Peter's time, but I also worked to garner more regularly the wisdom of those church people who had agreed to be an ad hoc group of advisors when my first quarter-time contract was signed. I could see that the conversion of that group into a more active advisory committee *ahora fue necesario* (was now essential) if Puente Ministry were to build a strong, sustainable organization and funding base. Through all this, my first concern was to be sure that our services to the men would continue, as I knew they would both benefit from and become leaders for the new workers to follow.

One of the first to volunteer for that advisory committee was one of the retired pastors in our Sunday preaching rotation, Rev. Ted. He told me he was particularly interested in Puente Ministry because he knew firsthand what it was like to be a stranger in an unfamiliar country. He had been a pastor in Germany for many years—serving two congregations, one on either side of the Berlin Wall—and he had gone to that country not speaking German very fluently. From the beginning of Puente Ministry, he was a passionate voice on the advisory committee, and later he became a faithful member of Puente's Board of Directors. Rev. Ted was indeed the spiritual leader of the Puente Ministry from its beginning until he retired in June of 2007.

Diane, the church bookkeeper, agreed to be on the advisory committee and to keep a record of the donations and expenses of Puente. Barbara, my mentor and former ESL teacher, also sat on the committee, as did Jill, a local veterinarian. Carol, a long-time community activist and executive director of North Street Family Resource Center, rounded out this group of five. It was a completely voluntary group—all church members and all deeply interested in the well-being of the men.

Right from the beginning, I had made a point to talk with this group as questions came up, as new possibilities for service were suggested, or as problems arose. Often *su punto de vista* (their insight and perspective) or *su sabiduría* (their wisdom) was just what I needed to navigate a challenging situation. Now I would formalize that contact through more regular meetings, official reports, and solid discussions about future plans.

The Ladies' Guild of the church also provided that kind of steadfast support from the outset. Over and over they proved they could be counted on to quickly provide whatever was needed—as I found out one evening when Cirino, one of the younger men, had a bicycle accident *en las curvas* (on the curvy part) of Bean Hollow Road. It happened shortly after the shoulder on that road had been repaired—and while the asphalt still had a sharp drop-off. He took a fall directly on his upper arm and smashed it badly. A passerby called for the paramedics. As they treated him, he told them that he didn't want to leave the immediate area, and so they took him to the only emergency room on the coast, the one in Montara.

After his injury was treated, Cirino was told that his arm would require further surgery at the County Hospital in San Mateo. But he had no money to pay the required $300 deposit for the surgery. Although he did have a sister living in the area, she did not have a legal driver's license, nor money to help him.

It was a Saturday evening when he came to our back door. We shared a cup of tea and he cried as he told me what was happening. The next day, I prayed aloud for him in church—and immediately the president of the Ladies' Guild contacted the other women in the group and arranged for a check to cover the deposit.

Ellen and I were headed on vacation the next day, which was also the day Cirino was to see the surgeon, and so we took the check to the hospital's admitting office on our way out of town. Ray made sure that Cirino got to the right place and saw the proper doctor. Through Ellen's work at the County Health Department, we were able to check that the proper paperwork was in place and that Cirino would be accepted for surgery. Later, one doctor commented in passing that had Cirino delayed another day or two, his arm might have developed gangrene badly enough to need amputation. Blessings abound!

That was not the last gracious act by our Ladies' Guild. Again and again, these women showed their support and desire to serve the poorest of the poor in our community. Whether ordering ESL books and earphones, or Spanish-language and bilingual Bibles, these women rose to meet the needs of Puente Ministry as well as various wider community and international missions.

As word began to spread of the "bridge-building" taking place in Pescadero, many people in church began leaving checks for Puente in the offering plate. Once the offering was counted and the Puente money separated out, Denise, one of the women in Ladies'Guild, would handwrite thank-you notes acknowledging each gift for Puente. And Diane, the volunteer bookkeeper for the church, would use the Puente money to pay the bills for the blankets, rice, beans, diapers, or reflectors I bought. During the first year or two, all the financial transactions were handled in this careful, though informal way.

As the months flowed by, we even began to receive support from the wider community outside Pescadero. Friends in the Belmont church had followed our progress with interest, and contributions came in from both individuals and the congregation's mission fund. Long-time friends from the East Bay church where I had been a seminary intern invited me to come and talk about what we were doing, and soon they were sending checks, too.

Each check deserved, and for tax purposes required, an acknowledgement. Plus, I truly wanted to thank each one personally. But as much as my heart yearned to write each donor a thoughtful note in my own handwriting, neither Denise nor I could keep up with this task. And so the stack grew. Finally after months of moaning, Margaret stopped me in my tracks.

"Let's just enter all of them in a database and get those letters out!" she said. Thanks be to God for many gifts, one spirit! Margaret's presence of peace and patience was just what we needed at that time. It is easy to become overwhelmed; but we uphold each other along the way.

The following week when we met for lunch, I handed Margaret a bundle of envelopes and a sheaf of legal paper full of notes with the names, addresses, and donations provided to Puente. As she entered each person into the database, she invited me to type in a personal note. It was only a sentence or two, and it often included something unique to the current agricultural season, and an invitation to come visit Puente. That got the job done!

In a very short time, we had a neat pile of envelopes containing appropriate thank-you letters all stamped and ready for me to drop in the post box. After that I regularly brought bundles of donation information to Margaret, along with little notes about what I wanted to include in each letter, and a week later she would hand me a stack of letters to sign, fold, stamp and mail. Through Peter's creativity with Filemaker and database programming, that simple database became the seed for Puente's full-blown donor database.

Always there was more to do—more blankets to buy, more people needing assistance or advocacy, and for this we needed money. We knew that when people heard the stories of what we were doing, they responded. If we were to meet more of the men's needs, we had to communicate our "wish list" and explain the realities of work in Pescadero to a wider audience.

I found myself telling the Puente story over and over to anyone who would listen. I told of seeing the lonely men around the edges of our community, and of knowing in my heart that these were "the strangers" spoken of in Matthew, strangers whom we are admonished to serve as we would serve the Christ. What an opportunity! A life of integrity with our faith and principles! I had read that scripture all my life, but here and now I had the experience of living it.

As personal donations increased, as an ever-increasing number of faith communities added Puente to their outreach giving, and as our first foundation grants came in, I realized that we needed a full-blown budget. I knew very little about creating *presupuestos* (budgets) since my work had been as a pastor and teacher, but Margaret had served as a school district business manager for many years before retiring and entering her current business. It was clear to both of us that we needed to work out a thoughtful budget process, establish our own bookkeeping system, and open a bank account.

Margaret brought up an Excel spreadsheet, and we began to chart out the categories of expenses we now had. On another spreadsheet, we plotted the income we had received and expected to receive. Once we established a bank account and began receiving regular bank statements, we were able to create accurate reports of our financial status. We also began to prepare reports projecting what we could expect for the next month, or six months.

Then we created a complete annual spending plan that included the costs of actual salary and benefits, and various kinds of insurance. Drawing on her years of experience, Margaret knew how to proceed. It wasn't long until she set up our whole plan in QuickBooks and began to provide official reports to our advisory committee. These reports became necessary as we responded to our foundation grantors.

However, day-to-day bookkeeping was not Margaret's favorite thing, and so we began to look for a part-time staff person in town who was qualified and willing to take over this role. Fortunately, Emily, the daughter of the executive director of South Coast Children's Services, had recently returned to town after a long absence—and she was looking for work! The best part was that while she was away, she had trained as a bookkeeper and was truly a professional in that area. Just what we needed! Margaret gladly turned over her files, and from that point Emily handled our financial recordkeeping, later adding a payroll service as our staff numbers increased.

With the donation acknowledgments, banking and financial planning now working well, we turned our attention to publicity. How were we to tell the story to a wider audience?

I shared the Puente story with my former Belmont church very early on. Like most United Church of Christ congregations, Belmont's congregation was liberal, upper middle class, predominantly white, and justice-seeking. And church members prided themselves on "outreach" giving: they had for many years raised substantial sums of money to distribute among a half-dozen local groups ministering to the poor. But until I became involved with Puente, they had not considered contributing to a ministry serving Mexican agricultural workers: they simply had no personal contact with such workers anywhere on the Mid-Peninsula. Now they, too, were beginning to get it.

> We see because we have been seen;
> We love because we have been loved.

> —Cynthia Anderson
> in "Christian Century," January 13, 2009

I began to speak more frequently at different churches in the area, and once I got to know our Spanish brothers better, they began *me acompañaban* (to accompany me) when I spoke. Gabriel and Mauricio, our "regulars," reveled in handing out newsletters and joining the after-worship meals with mission boards and deacons. This was a very personal way to get the story out, a "hands-on" immersion experience for people in these new communities *que no vivían dentro de nuestro compañerismo ni nuestra experiencia* (who were outside our fellowship and experience).

Clearly, we also needed to create some printed materials. Margaret told me I needed a statement describing just what Puente was trying to do, and so we sat down to draft one. I carried it back to the Puente advisory committee and they contributed their thoughts. Finally, Puente's first mission statement *llegó a ser así* (emerged): *Building bridges of understanding between the Spanish-speaking and English-speaking peoples of Pescadero, making resources available to all.*

The best part was that those bridges were actually growing more substantial as more English-speakers enrolled in Spanish classes and began to be able to talk with the men in their own language. As more men came to *La Sala* each week and practiced speaking with English-speaking friends, their confidence grew, too. Other ESL teachers and people from our faith community brought food and stayed to play dominoes. The Second Harvest enrollment and regular food distribution continued to make resources available to more people. And transportation to the Mexican Consulate, doctors, dentists, and optometrists was becoming easier for the men to obtain.

In spite of this growth in understanding, sometimes we still failed to "get it." One day, Alfredo told me he could not "see." I arranged for him to see the eye doctor in Half Moon Bay, and he actually went. After a thorough exam, the doctor told him he had excellent vision. Ultimately, I came to understand that he meant he could not "read." The trip to the eye doctor was not the issue, but learning to read Spanish was! Again, I was reminded to practice listening, rather than assuming I knew what was best for another. This is the direction in which God is calling us as we serve others.

To be sure that everyone we met knew how to access the ministry, we needed something to give them. I was delighted when Margaret showed me the brochure she had created for their business, and I knew we needed a similar handout for Puente. The annual conference of the Northern

California/Nevada UCC churches was coming up soon, and most of the 120 churches would be attending. It became our goal to create a brochure for that conference that would tell the Puente story.

The brochure's cover had to grab the reader's attention and say: *This is about agricultural workers and ministry.* And we had to have a bridge, of course, something like the bridge in the redwoods on the poster I had carried with me since seminary days.

Margaret and I had already gone through dozens of clip-art when we were designing the letterhead for our database-generated thank-you letters. We had looked at bridges and pictures of bridges, but nothing was quite right. In the end, we had assembled a homemade logo for our letterhead using the letters *PUENTE* curved in the shape of a bridge.

Margaret had also come up with a figure of a man with a big hat holding a potted plant. This became our face for "The Men Alone." And we had asked permission of a beloved church woman and local artist, Denise Marks, to use the woodcut she created which showed the front view of the Pescadero church.

We rearranged these three elements to form the cover design for our first brochure—a simple tri-folded piece of paper. We included an excerpt of Scripture: *I was a stranger and you took me in. You fed, clothed, and visited me... .*[9] And the cover was complete, wrapped in God's love.

The purpose of our brochure was to tell our story—and to enlist donations, volunteers, and interest. On one inside panel, we listed the ways Puente served the community. On another, which featured a tall redwood tree, we displayed the names of the faith communities in which our ministry was rooted. We made sure people knew that these communities contributed half of the income necessary to keep the ministry going.

We highlighted "bikes, blankets and beans" as the basic items we distributed. A short paragraph (frequently updated) tallied distributed items to date. We also described the "blessing of the bikes," with a picture showing how my mentor, the late Reverend Dan Aprá, and I had prayed over the men and bikes at the distribution gathering at the church. And we included information on *La Sala*—its hours, location, and the varied activities offered there.

Of course, the brochure invited the reader to check off the ways in which he or she might want to volunteer or donate, and included a form to collect names and mailing information.

Once we had completed the design, Margaret took the brochure to the local copy shop and ran two-sided copies on bright green paper. The green symbolized for us both community growth and prolific crops. Later we would run brochures by the thousands, but that first print run was about 150 copies—just enough for me to take to the Northern California/Nevada UCC conference. Margaret also printed up my first batch of business cards using the inexpensive, pre-perforated card stock that was popular then. We had made our deadline!

Once we got to the conference, Ellen and I registered and then sat down and folded the brochures ourselves. I set up a table for Puente and laid out our new brochures, business cards, a sample of our welcome bags (fully-stuffed), and binders full of

---

[9] Matthew 25:35 (paraphrased)

photos showing things we were doing alongside local media clippings.

I had also been asked to conduct *un taller* (a workshop) about Puente. During my workshop, I explained the working and living situations in Pescadero, and I described the farms and ranches. I talked about the crops—*cebolla, esprados, guisantes, alstromeria, lilias, estock, albahaca, romero, tomillo y setas* (onions, Brussels sprouts, peas, Peruvian lilies, Cala lilies, stock, basil, rosemary, thyme and mushrooms). I explained that much of the soil had been depleted, and some of the growers were shifting from field crops to specialty items, such as herbs or fava beans, to reintroduce nitrogen into the fields. Crops that had once been profitable in the area—roses, daisies, strawflowers, and artichokes—were no longer grown, I explained, because other countries—Colombia, Mexico, Chile—had taken over those markets, causing a few local growers and ranchers to retire or go bankrupt.

I included some brief notes about the geographic and economic conditions along the south coast and interior of Mexico, the states from which most of the men had come—Oaxaca, Guanajuato, Jalisco, Mexico, Sierra León. I tried to put a real face on these men who came desperate for dollars to send back to their families, yet longing to be home. Their heartache had been made worse by the alienation they felt: for the fifteen years before Puente got started, only a handful of people had called them by name.

Workshop attendees, lay and clergy alike, began to understand how important bikes were to the men. They also empathized with our desire to provide the men with blankets and warm sweatshirts. But, it was hard for my "privileged" peers to imagine anyone in these times living in a situation where they would lack water for washing and drinking, where neither public nor private bathroom facilities would be open to them, where a hot meal would be a special treat. Those who most quickly related to the men's stories were a group of Japanese families whose relatives had been laborers or farmers swept up and forced to live in internment camps during WWII.

Ironically, Pescadero had been home to one of those camps in the '40s—situated right on Bean Hollow Road.

From this conference, I received additional invitations to speak at the home churches of the various attendees. Friends of Puente also recommended my presentations to women's clubs in the Presbyterian Church and in other denominational gatherings. And the planners of the UCC National Rural Initiative asked me to speak at their gathering in the Franklinton Center in South Carolina.

The brochure and my speaking engagements brought more donations and more volunteers to our work in Pescadero. Now it was time to create a brochure in Spanish, explaining to the men the services generated by all this goodwill.

That second brochure, which came quickly after the first, was designed to be visually clear for the workers who might not be literate. We found simple icons to represent the services available to the men—where to find restrooms, how to call the fire department, where to get emergency medical services, how to get to the clinic, and how to enroll in ESL classes. And we began distributing these brochures as widely as possible.

And when previous donors and volunteers began calling and asking *what else* they could do to help, we decided we also needed a newsletter. One of our board members offered to fund a local artist who would create a professional logo for the newsletter. With a dozen meetings and color schemes, multiple trips over the hill to her place in San Carlos and revisions, it came to pass. This logo, the artist said, was designed to carry the idea *that they may all be one.*[10] One body, imagine!

---

[10] John 17:11

Our brochures, our newsletter, and my speaking invitations were rapidly spreading the Puente story around the San Francisco Bay Area. As I talked with people in distant towns, they'd often ask, "Now, where is Pescadero? Where are all those farms where the men work?" or "I've lived here all my life, and I've never seen nurseries, ranches or workers. Oh, but Duarte's Tavern and Restaurant, I've been there many times!"

And so, of course, we also decided we needed to create a map—a visual representation of the ranches and farms we were talking so much about. We wanted people to *see* what had been hidden for so long.

Margaret brought up a drawing program on her computer screen, and using a map of the Coast that we found on the Internet, she traced the main roads around Pescadero, La Honda, San Gregorio, and Loma Mar. We placed *un corazón* (a heart symbol) at the location of each of these four unincorporated communities, and we added numbers to represent each farm, nursery, or living quarters that I could identify. *El clave* (the key) to the map listed the full names of each place. This map, which underwent many revisions, continued to serve for many years as a useful handout whenever I took a new person or group on our "reality tour."[11]

Who came on these tours? Our first group was composed of local church folks who had told me, "We've lived in Pescadero a very long time, and we don't even know where these ranches are. Will you take us out to see?" Then the Puente advisory committee requested a tour—and we quickly learned the wisdom of taking potential new members on tour before asking for a commitment to work on the Committee. Most of the volunteers at *La Sala* needed to know where the farms and ranches were located so they could take someone home or pick them up for Thanksgiving or Christmas. And reporters from the news media asked for tours when they were writing about farming and ranching in the area. People serving in governmental positions, including some from Board of Supervisors and aides to State representatives, came for tours.

---

[11] See map opposite Table of Contents in this book.

The managers of San Mateo County Public Health and County Social Services spent a full day on tour to better understand how and whom they served. Emergency medical personnel asked for a tour. The schoolteachers of our district toured annually with new staff members. Sierra Club and other conservation groups, individual donors, youth groups, bike donors, churchwomen's groups, and social action clubs all called to schedule tours.

Every program officer from the various foundations that supported Puente received a site visit, as did the funders of our sister agencies in town. Groups from agencies seeking to do similar work in other rural areas came to glean what they could from our model. Billie, one of our interns from Pacific School of Religion, brought the Stanford Urban Ministries international fellows to see rural realities. It was a perfect teachable moment, an opportunity to let people see for themselves how the workers lived in and around our small farms and nurseries.

So it was that through our brochures, our newsletter, and even an area map, we carried the story of the Puente Ministry to people both in our local community and throughout the greater Bay Area. And when people heard our stories, they responded. They gave us donations, and they gave us their presence and energies. And Puente Ministry blossomed.

9

Working with Adult Volunteers

In everyone there is the capacity
to wake up,
to understand
and to love.

— Thich Nhat Hanh, *Being Peace*

We are admonished in *las escrituras* (the Scriptures), *you shall love your neighbor as yourself,*[12] and many of us struggle with this passage: we find it difficult to love ourselves, let alone to love—or even to know—*nuestros vecinos* (our neighbors). But in Puente Ministry, right from the beginning, Scripture was lived out. Puente Ministry seemed to attract an amazing number of people who were genuinely filled with the longing to be good neighbors.

As our Ministry grew, volunteers came to Puente in increasing numbers. Some came because they knew me casually: they were members of my local women's exercise class, or students from Spanish class, or congregants from church. Some came because of what they heard about the Ministry while enjoying waffles and pancakes at the community's monthly

---

[12] Mark 12:31

breakfast in fellowship hall. A few Puente regulars brought their favorite maple syrup to share with strangers, adding yet another gesture of welcome.

Several Puente volunteers I had originally met on Main Street or at the post office. Others had heard about Puente by word of mouth from friends. The woman who owned my workout gym rallied our "gym rat" friends to donate jackets and make contributions; I often overheard her talking up the food program or recruiting additional volunteers. Folks came down from Half Moon Bay, up from Santa Cruz, or over the hill from San Carlos.

As people heard the Puente story, they often asked to come to Pescadero and be a part of what was happening. Friends from our former Belmont church happily took over the preparation of the Thanksgiving meal at *La Sala* each November. They brought in turkeys with all the trimmings; ordered tamales and locally prepared rice and beans; and carried along incredible quantities of canned goods and fruit for the men to take home. The crew bustled for hours in the big kitchen of Native Sons' Hall, often with local volunteers. Everyone worked together making sure all the food was hot and ready by the time the men arrived at four o'clock. When the men arrived, they greeted each one with a special welcome at this holiday feast. Then they made sure that each man got as many full plates as he wanted. Most of the men dutifully and graciously ate the *pavo y papas* (turkey and mashed potatoes) with gravy, *habichuelas verdes* (green beans) and *pastel de calabaza* (pumpkin pie) offered to them, but the tamales, homemade by our friend Guadalupe, were the dish of choice.

When the meal was over, any food left was carefully packaged so that the men could *llevar para compartir* (take a portion to share) with those who hadn't been brave enough to come or who had been required to work that day. Thanksgiving is not a Latino holiday, but the men are generally given the whole day off each year. Later the Belmont volunteers told me how they would return home buzzing with stories, glowing with the light of the fellowship, and vowing to sign on for next year.

Their inspiration came from an Old Testament prophet:

What does the Lord require of you:
To seek justice and love kindness
And walk humbly with your God.

— Micah 6:8

But getting to Pescadero for the feast could be a challenge for the men. The local bus company—SamCoast—was contractually unable to work on Thanksgiving, and so the men had to find their own ways to our celebration. During one particularly wet holiday, a family whose wife I had buried the previous Christmas came out to help. *El viudo, su hija, y yerno* (the widower, his daughter and son-in-law) all volunteered to take separate vehicles *para buscarles a los hombres que no tenían ni carros ni amigos que se lleven* (to find men who did not have cars or buddies to bring them) the miles into town. Another volunteer and her husband brought blankets for the workers, and we added sweatshirts and socks, which we had in our larder. It was *un año rico* (a rich year) for us all.

People who volunteered felt so good about being here that they wanted to share the experience with their friends and relatives. We began to invite our families from St. Louis, Portland, Seattle and Vancouver to meet up at *La Sala* for the Thanksgiving and Christmas meals each year. Townspeople came to the elementary school gymnasium to offer their time and energy during the Second Harvest food distribution. Students earned their Community Service hours by volunteering with us. Even the middle-school kids from South Coast Children's Services would begin their after school activities by packing food boxes. Folks often told me these tasks were the most tangible and satisfying work in town. We all loved to help each other out. We loved being good neighbors. And like my mom used to say, "Many hands make light work. "

And so wherever I happened to be, I would look for ways to meet new people and to tell them what was going on in

Pescadero. One opportunity came in the year 2000, when I worked on the U.S. Census in the Pescadero region. My service area included the ranches where the workers lived, and the houses along the Coast Highway, some of which were weekend or vacation homes. When I talked to Lilia, the North Street administrator, about taking the training necessary for becoming a census worker, she suggested that her young adult brother, Saul, take the training. Accompanied by Saul I gained credibility among the Spanish-speaking population and was able to gather data from many people who might otherwise have not opened their door to me.

In a place like Pescadero, folks are easily identified by their vehicles, and so I always scanned the parked cars along Stage Road and in the post office lot to see who was in town. One day during this period when I was at the post office, I spotted an unfamiliar, dark brown Subaru Forester with a bright rainbow sticker on it. As the driver emerged from the post office, I stepped forward and introduced myself. I found out that she—Kerry—had recently rented a home near Bean Hollow Beach, in my census area.

Of course, I knew the house. It had been built some years earlier by the Rev. Ted and his son. He and his wife had recently sold it and moved to Half Moon Bay. Now Kerry would be living there. In a small community, we know each other's stories, and we keep track of how we are interconnected.

During our conversation, Kerry asked me if I might recommend someone who could house- and pet-sit for her when she had to work out of the area.

I said, "Sure, I know lots of people. I'd be glad to check for you."

Later that week, Kerry and I found time for a little afternoon tea. We discovered that we had mutual friends in the United Fellowship of Metropolitan Community Churches and among her coastside Jewish community. By the time our tea was cold, we had shared our common passion for community organizing and our concern for issues of justice.

Then Kerry asked if I would do the house- and pet-sitting. She knew it was likely that a pastor and her partner could use a night or two of "sabbatical retreat" on the ocean—keeping company with Kerry's two beloved cats, Lucky and Annie, and her dog, Buddy. Kerry and I both thought it was a match made in heaven. That arrangement lasted, on and off, for three years.

Over time, Kerry became the lead volunteer for our food program, found bikes for us, and coached me in the ways of becoming an executive director as Puente grew. Her understanding of Spanish, her care for the brothers, and her devotion to doing justice work became strong points of attachment that bonded her deeply to our local community ministry.

Although I regularly worshiped at Pescadero Community Church, from time to time I walked up North Street to St. Anthony's and shared information about Puente's services during the announcements at mass. I told the congregants about the availability of resources, or flu immunizations, or HIV/AIDS testing. And often Fr. Medina and I would rush out after mass to the mobile clinic in the St. Anthony's social hall to receive the first two shots, or medical tests, in hopes that others would follow our lead. Together we had a great Christian community, with our two tiny parishes around the corner from one another—two missions serving the people on the Coast. This spirit of cooperation was wonderful. After Fr. Medina was reassigned, we continued making connections through the Catholic Worker House in Half Moon Bay. And sometimes people I met at St. Anthony's would drop in as volunteers for Puente.

Jim and Genevieve were one of those couples. At that time, they were worshipping primarily with Fr. Medina at St. Anthony's—and only occasionally at the community church. Ellen and I often attended High Holy Day or Saturday night Spanish masses at St. Anthony's, and we would sometimes meet them as we were leaving those services. When they attended the community church services, we'd sometimes share Sunday lunch locally. It may have been the monthly community pancake breakfast at our church that first drew Jim and Gen into our midst.

Whatever first attracted them, Jim and Gen became another amazing resource for Puente. Early on, they volunteered to become over-the-hill shoppers for Puente. Gen also began working with the children at North Street, and both enrolled in my community-wide Spanish classes. Jim progressed quickly, and soon began using his childhood Spanish name *"Jaime"* from his days growing up in the *barrios* (neighborhoods) of Southern California. He became a volunteer translator, and transporter, and mentor for our new staff outreach person. Together, Jaime and Gen brought many years of experience teaching and serving others to their work at Puente.

Lary and Rob, whom we met in Spanish class, lived near Jaime and Gen in the Butano Canyon enclave, and they, too, became friends of Puente. When they told me that many of their neighbors had been hiring Mexican nationals for years, we enlisted their help in spreading the word about Puente. Soon, because of their contacts, Butano Canyon residents began to hire the men who were part of Puente. They trusted our referrals, and they were glad to have our brothers in their gated sanctuary—so much so that the community became known as "Puente South."

Other Butano Canyon connections also benefited Puente. When someone in Butano Canyon moved away, friends would often bring leftover food and furniture to be distributed to the ranches or used at *La Sala*. Carol and her husband, Paul, also from the Canyon, became Puente volunteers. Carol soon took over the coordination of food distribution and the donor database, which Margaret greatly appreciated. Later when they decided to retire to the Northwest, Carol groomed Nancy to take her place in the food program. Succession planning is so important in any volunteer organization.

Carol, Nancy, Jaime and Gen managed the food drop-offs and repacking. Sometimes our volunteers included the workers themselves—such as *los Gabrieles* (the two Gabriels).

These men were happy to help especially when a situation arose for which their special talents were needed. Gabriel was a long-time friend from my early days standing on the steps of the church, and Gabi was a more recent arrival. What bounty we shared in the people resources, time and talents—all of which supported our mostly-volunteer ministry!

Our monthly food delivery from Second Harvest filled ten long tables that took up half the gym. And our list of recipients grew to more than a hundred workers, plus elders and disabled adults. Evelyn was one of those disabled elders. Each time as we approached her gate, her tiny dog jumped into action, barking ferociously as we gently talked our way past him. Once into the living room, we could greet her as she sat in her wheelchair smoking up a storm. She would offer us a "stiff drink," and when we declined, she would pour herself one and drink it while we unloaded groceries to the counter. There was no way she would let us put the groceries onto the shelves for her. No, sir! She would do that for herself, later. Before we left Evelyn always invited us to sit with her, and often she regaled us with a story or two about her life and her family.

We also delivered food to hundreds of kids in the district's preschool, after-school and tutorial programs, plus another hundred children in summer school. I regularly drove out to the ranches to distribute leftover food. We let nothing go to waste.

One day Lary and Rob, who worked with community emergency services, told me that Pescadero had received a neighborhood grant from Peninsula Community Foundation to establish an emergency radio station. The station would broadcast weather warnings, road closures in times of flooding, and other emergency information. Twenty radios set to receive broadcasts on local station 1680 were to be distributed to workers living on the local ranches.

Lary and Rob had hired Mexican workers in the past, and both of them spoke enough Spanish to be comfortable overseeing the distribution of these radios. But they knew that the Spanish-speaking workers could describe the use of the radios more eloquently and convincingly than either of them. So Lary asked for volunteers from among the Puente men to assist in the distribution.

The workers who volunteered to take on this task already knew that some of the recipients would not be particularly interested. " 'God will take care of us,' " they told us the recipients would say: the confidence in God when faced with the possibility of fire, earthquake, flood or windstorm was pervasive in that Spanish-speaking community. Yet the brothers did their best to convince everyone *aprovecharse de* (to take advantage of) the radios. Since most workers did not have a radio new enough to receive the 1680 emergency frequency, these volunteers understood the importance of distributing this emergency equipment.

Partly because of his work distributing radios with the brothers, Lary began to find paying jobs for the brothers in homes located in the wider southcoast area, jobs the men sorely needed during the slack season. This was one of those wonderful "unintended consequences," a gift that was also fruit of their labor together.

Often, just when we needed a lift, a new volunteer would walk into the Ministry. This was certainly true of Fran, who appeared in worship one day with a joyful sense about her. Fran introduced herself by telling me she had been a rancher in Half Moon Bay in the 1950s. Recently, she had renewed her friendship with Duane, another nurseryman and friend from that period, who was still actively operating his place out on Cloverdale Road. Her days were divided between a home in the mountains and a modest beach house just north of town.

Fran confided in me that she came to her beach house in order to be close to her husband who was very ill and living in a care facility on the Peninsula. This made her our newest neighbor in the community—and once she joined the church, we became close. She even chose to be baptized! Since she regularly drove back and forth over the hill to visit her husband, she soon became one of our much-needed shoppers. She brought us *bolsas, jugo y palomitas* (sleeping bags, juice, and popcorn) and whatever else we lacked on the Coast.

As it happened, Fran's daughter had a teashop in San Carlos. One day while Fran and I were having a lunch there, one of the servers—Tiffany—overheard us discussing Puente. Immediately, she wanted to come and help. An undocumented immigrant from England herself, Tiffany knew full well the struggle of a border crossing and the limitations on her life in the United States. Tiffany did come over the hill for a year or more—for each Second Harvest distribution. Together with our new outreach worker, she carried deliveries to the ranches. She also built credibility with the men by listening to their stories, and telling them her own life stresses, which were not unlike theirs.

Fran also introduced me to her friend Jerry, who later contributed many winter jackets for the men. He also was a professional carpenter. This interest proved to be inspiring to some of our brothers who wanted to build and sell their products in town. But *desgraciadamente* (unfortunately), we could not find an available studio or shop where Jerry might teach the men what they needed to know. For lack of a place, we lost a chance to form a co-op and a sustainable cottage industry.

Perhaps this would happen later, we told ourselves, when housing for farm workers and low-income community professionals would be built in our area. We had already convened a community meeting during which we talked to both workers and teachers about the kinds of housing they needed, and we had discussed ways to use adjacent space for *juntas, jardines y talleres* (community gatherings, gardens and workshops). But even with the most stellar plans drawn up pro bono, even with artists and community activists working alongside the County Permit Office and the County Supervisors, we knew our project was not destined to happen quickly.

That's because it had taken some twenty years and a major effort to build low-income housing in Half Moon Bay. Finally, with the support of political representatives in Washington DC, that project had been funded—and an attractive, low-income housing development known as Moon Ridge had been built. The tenants and owners at Moon Ridge were limited to those working either in agriculture or the fishing industry. We kept the faith—and held onto the hope and plans for our project. Perhaps it will be completed sometime in the future.

Ed, who worked at the nursery in the foothills, was another angel for Puente. He made it his job to transport Franco home from *La Sala* each week. Ed knew that for Franco biking up *su colina* (his hill) at night was *muy peligroso* (extremely dangerous). Whenever Franco left *La Sala*, Ed would toss Franco's bike into the back of his truck and take him up the hill. When Ed had heart surgery at Sequoia Hospital, the brothers were eager to hear my updates on the progress of his healing, and the day he was released from the hospital, they welcomed him back at *La Sala* with gentle cheering. That evening Ed brought oranges or apples *para compartir* (to share) around the tables as he exchanged warm greetings with everyone.

Puente Ministry was bringing volunteers and workers together, but we always asked: What more could we do?

One day over our morning cups of hot tea, Ellen looked at me and said, "The HIV testing van is making a coastside run on Thursday. Would you like them to stop by *La Sala*?" It was a no brainer! Here I lived with my life partner who worked at the County Health Department AIDS Program—and I never thought to set up a testing opportunity for our men! What was I thinking?

On the following Thursday, the van rolled up and the staff jumped out eager to get started. But first we had to introduce the idea! Kathy, a Puente board member, told the men with my translation and a little tearfully, that if she were one of their wives, a sister, an aunt, a daughter or a mother, she would be so delighted to have them get this test—and treatment, if it were needed. She did not want them to die of AIDS, and she begged them *tomarlo en serio* (to consider this seriously).

Of course, there were the usual giggles when Laura, the AIDS outreach person, spoke clearly in Spanish of sexually transmitted diseases, and HIV/AIDS in particular. Miraculously, nineteen men agreed to the test that day, and in a week *cado uno de ellos* (each one of them) returned for his results. Of course, these results were totally confidential. I had no idea what the results were, but God willing, we persuaded some of the men to be more careful in any sexual encounter! From that day forward, they all picked up *condones* (condoms) from *la canasta en el baño* (the basket in the bathroom) at *La Sala*.

Ellen told me later that when a group is tested, it is rare to have this kind of response. But it was clear that the men were growing to trust Puente. And for the Ministry, this was another demonstration of our commitment to offer sound health care information in Spanish to all.

10

Adding Young People

Ultimately, we have just one moral duty:
to reclaim large areas of peace in ourselves,
more and more peace,
and reflect it towards others.

— Etty Hillesum, *An Interrupted Life:
The Journal of a Young Jewish Woman, 1941-1943*

Not only did we involve lots of men and women in Puente Ministry, we also attracted many young people. And they brought their youthful energies, inquiring minds, and new ideas with them.

It started with a request from a Santa Cruz UCC church to bring a group of junior high youth for a service project. *¡Cómo no!* (Of course!) What a gift to have the time and talents of such an energetic group! They assembled, labeled, and stamped Puente newsletters. They painted fences at the goat farm with the farm owner, who was also a community organizer, local school supporter, and my dear friend. And they sorted jewelry and greeting cards with Cleotilde, a local mom, who was also a good friend of mine. The jewelry and cards were then sold at *La Pulguita* (the Little Flea market), the South Coast Children's Services-youth-sponsored thrift shop that Cleotilde managed. Groups of kids from that same church came for several years, donating an afternoon's work each time, bringing a few repaired bikes, and often ending with a beach outing.

A group of senior high youth from First Congregational Church of Berkeley UCC came, too, with their sponsors. They wanted to offer *gratis* (absolutely free) a weeklong day camp in June for all the five- to nine-year-olds we could enroll. The children in this age group rarely had opportunities for organized summer fun. We were both surprised and delighted.

We sent out flyers to the families with children in school explaining who would be *en cargado de todo* (in charge) of their children, what they would be doing, when, and where. Twenty names appeared quickly on the sign-up sheets. With the gracious assistance of Norka, our local preschool teacher, we quickly translated a boilerplate version of the school's parent permission slips, sent them out, and were amazed with the immediate response. We had the signed slips in hand long before the deadline. This parent group was ready to participate fully on behalf of their children. What a gratifying time in the life of our town to see the mostly Spanish-speaking parents so very supportive of our new activities, trusting their children to Puente and to a group of "strangers from across the Bay."

The youth group came with their sponsors and all their gear to lead the kids through standard camp activities. The youth worked out the camp program, brought all the supplies and food, and handled all the activities. They sang songs, played games, made chalk art on the church parking lot, did crafts, offered snacks and made new friends. We shuttled them on well-chaperoned field trips to the beach. Whether the activity included Frisbee throwing, crab watching, sand castle building, hiking, or chasing each other in and out of the gathering "pools" by the caves, everyone loved the fresh air and freewheeling fun.

At night the teens slept in their sleeping bags on the church floor, in the pews, and around the chancel area. After the little children were delivered home each day, I met with the youth to share their reflections and to lead them in silent meditation. It was a teachable moment for social justice, for

U.S./Mexico border issues, and for Mexican culture in the true context of hands-on ministry.

During this time we were able to arrange for the children to swim at a nearby pool. What a *don* (kind gift) from the live-in caretakers, Judy and Bert! Judy, who directed the South Coast Children's Services in our village, clearly knew what the kids liked. The two adults were even able to provide *el guardavidas* (a lifeguard) to protect the children! After a quick round up of extra swimsuits for those who did not have them, and shorts for those too bashful to don a suit, we set out for the pool. Volunteers gave a new towel to each child, which they were allowed to take home. With much laughter and giggling, we got nearly every child into the water. With some we simply held hands and jumped in together, while with others we sat on the steps and dangled our toes.

Another local mom, Kellie, who for decades organized the annual Pescadero Arts and Fun Fest youth booths, arranged for a hike, a campfire, and a nature talk from a park ranger in an area that is normally off limits. Again, we felt a great debt of gratitude to Kellie for arranging these extraordinary, extravagant gifts. What a visit! The children played joyfully, and justice was well served. What more could one ask for in summer?

On the last day of summer camp, the children's *familias* (families) brought to the church lavish *bonches de flores* (bunches of flowers), bouquets even more profuse than the bunches often shared with the youthful drivers when they dropped off their charges at the end of the day. Sometimes, this is what gratitude looks like in an agri/floriculture community: a profusion of color and fragrance as *gracias* (thanks-giving).

That following *Navidad* (Christmas), these same young people returned for a campers' reunion. They filled every pew in the church with *juguetes, libros y ropa* (toys, books and clothes) for Christmas "shopping" by parents, while their children were distracted and adoringly entertained and fed by the youth. There were skates, skateboards, construction kits, bilingual books, bedding, warm clothes, boots, and toys of every variety.

145

The young people had certainly brought an "extravagant welcome to strangers" from their own church members. In a few hours, parents' large black plastic bags were *bien llenas* (completely stuffed) with gifts; *no había ni sobras* (nothing was left over) in the pews.

Another summer we hosted a group of young people from a church in Madison, Wisconsin, who came for a service retreat. They planned to focus on silent spiritual practices along with their service experience. Why kids from Wisconsin, you might ask? A pastor friend of mine from Fresno and his family had been called to serve "back home" in the Midwest, and his co-pastor was looking for a service trip with a spirit of mission for their youth during summer vacation. They, along with an equal number of adults, wanted to learn how to balance faith and justice. These visitors came to see firsthand how we were faithfully bridging the gaps between Spanish-speakers and English-speakers in our community.

These youngsters also camped out in the church by night, and by day we balanced a contemplative and silent meditation practice with a curriculum developed to include faith and action, scripture, singing, and daily discussions of economic realities both in Mexico and on our local farms or ranches.

Margaret and I assembled a booklet of activities and Spanish phrases and vocabulary[13] for the young people to use during their stay with us, and to take home later. We also created a first-night scavenger hunt designed to familiarize these young people with the lack of facilities and resources in town. And we included articles about Mexican culture, economics, sociology, history and religious practices. On the final pages we described the current immigrant situation in this country, including border-crossing difficulties.

Every morning we practiced silent-walking meditation— on the beach, down Main Street, along the edges of plowed and planted fields, or inside the sanctuary. The young people drilled

---

[13] For a copy, contact the authors via www.no-longer-strangers.org.

each other on common Spanish phrases, completed work projects around Pescadero, and played soccer with the men after everyone's work was complete.

There was time to work at *La Pulguita*, to milk the goats and to clean the goat barns, to plant and weed the organic flowers that would later be used in packaging *queso de cabras* (the goat cheese), and to tour the cheese factory. There was time to sort and stack the clothing they had brought to share— sweatshirts, jackets, socks, T-shirts—and to organize a giveaway. And in between, there was just enough time for showers *cada otro día* (every other day) at either the goat farm or community members' homes before *la cena* (supper).

During their week with us, the youth shared several meals with the men. At those times, all of us heard firsthand stories of border crossings and families left behind. Antonio and two others shared stories of *el uso y abuso de alcohol y drogas* (the use and abuse of alcohol and drugs) within their community, ending with stories of their own recoveries.

One day we were all invited to attend *el bautizo* (the baptism) celebration of José, one young Spanish-speaking man who worked at one of the ranches along with his wider family. The family invited about fifty of his friends to a ranch just outside of town where they lived and worked. We all enjoyed *un bienvenido típico* (a welcome typical) of family celebrations in Mexico. It included *una barbacoa de pollo, hamburguesas y carne de res* (barbequed chicken, hamburgers, and beef steaks) with *tamales y bebidas* (tamales and non-alcoholic drinks). Most festive of all was our friend José, dressed up in *un traje y corbata* (a suit and tie)!

On that day, the Midwesterners went home with a few more Spanish phrases, a broader understanding of Mexican culture, and personal experience of the extravagant welcome to *los estranjeros* (the strangers). And this time, *we* were the strangers—the ones invited into the Mexican community to socialize with The Men Alone and the families on that ranch. That day we accepted each other and trusted in one incarnate family, the hope of all community-building.

Toward the end of their visit, one of the Midwestern youth told me he was aware of growing numbers of Spanish-speaking men and women working in service industries in Madison. He went on to say that Mexican residents were not very visible to most people in town, and there was little, if any, cooperative or collaborative outreach from the English-speaking, urban community. It was evident to him that his church in Madison could find ways to step up and make a difference. But how were they to take this experience back to their parents, some of whom were not of one accord regarding the Mexican population in this nation, let alone their own community? More reason for the walking centering meditation in which we engaged in California.

The Puente experience enriched not only the lives of hundreds of adult volunteers and teenagers on service retreats, it also offered practical training for seminary interns. We were blessed during those early community-building years with two interns. These young women were enormously helpful on the preaching rotation at the church, and they provided a powerful camaraderie for me: I was no longer alone in this mission of serving our beloved community.

Our first full-year intern, Billie, was a Pacific School of Religion student who applied to spend a year in practical training with both the Pescadero church/Puente Ministry and Stanford University. She had grown up in California in a farm worker family, and she brought with her a gentle compassion rooted in her Mexican heritage. She knew firsthand from *sus tíos* (her uncles) the uncertain plight the men faced in fieldwork. Her demeanor with Anglos and Mexican workers alike was kind, solid, sensitive and pastoral.

Despite the fact that Billie already understood almost all the Spanish that was spoken around her, she ached to be able to speak Spanish with more comfort. This woman was the first person in her family to graduate from a university and the first person to earn a Masters in Divinity at seminary. Her own experience with her college-aged son brought a certain expertise and understanding to life with The Men Alone. While she was with us, she often brought international students from Stanford to our *La Sala* meetings, to our food distributions, and to tours of our farms and ranches. This was an eye-opener for the students, many of whom came from urban setting and knew little of their own countries' agricultural industries or workers' lives. As they got to know Pescadero and the men, they often redeemed their campus food coupons for treats to bring to the men, and downloaded Mexican music on their laptops to share with them. Later Billie took these same students on a border immersion-experience across the U.S. Southwest—through Arizona, New Mexico, and Texas.

The following year, a second intern came from Pacific School of Religion. Monique, or "Moni" as we called her, worked with us for ten to fifteen hours a week, becoming a Puente regular at *La Sala* and at the church. She had worked for KDTV, a Bay Area TV channel, as an announcer. The men were dazzled by her striking Mexican style, and her fluent Spanish. Her life before we met had clearly been lived in the privileged class. As a child, she had been brought up with servants, as was appropriate for the daughter of a well-to-do Mexico City businessman and rancher. Her college education at the University of Arizona and her travels to Italy with her former husband and kids had further enriched her experience. While both her education and upper-class status might have set her apart, Moni's basic kindness and obvious compassion carried her into our hearts. The presence at *La Sala* of her two young children, her mother, and her brother often called up for the men comforting memories of pleasant times at home.

As I mentored these two very special women in church polity, in wedding and funeral services, in ways to serve in traditional church, and in street ministry, I often reflected on their youthfulness and their new pastoral callings in relation to my own work. I had been the founding pastor for Puente; now I was the stalwart, nearly-retirement-aged staff person—someone the men had come to count on as a kind of the *abuelita* (grandmother). Together we three women sang different and wondrous parts in a harmonious song of compassionate response.

In earlier days, Moni had worked in a street ministry, and she was very familiar with the homeless. One day, when she met Johnnie Angel on the road outside of town, she persuaded him to come with her to church! After that she took a special interest in him and got him to stick around a bit more than I had ever done. On those occasions when Johnnie was with us, he took to fashioning "life story walking canes" for both the newcomers and longtime parishioners at church. As he chatted with a person, he seemed to take note of the milestones in their personal history. Then, he would select a stick and attached something that symbolized those important events or episodes. He had in his bag quite a cache of bits and pieces he had collected as he walked. Using recycled items, he created objects of art, and the colorful effects were quite dazzling. His handiwork was always amazing and distinctly his own.

Both Moni and I plied him with fresh clothes, which he sometimes took and other times declined. We both tried to interest him in eating, but rarely found him willing to join us for a meal or snack. A few times, he did stop by *La Sala* and traded stories with the men. His heritage seemed to be a mixture of Italian and Puerto Rican, and he spoke both Spanish and English with ease, and could speak with Moni in Spanish, English or a little Italian. Clearly, he had attended schools in his youth and was well-informed on a wide range of topics.

During that time, Johnnie was another "stranger" and not always well received. Some in town looked at him and turned the other way. Others wondered what he was doing at "our" church—and said so in public. He was often a bit smelly, his clothes were hardly pristine, and he lived a very different life on the road. But to their surprise, as they got to know him, they discovered that he was also a wonderfully gifted soul. One Sunday when he happened to be in church, Moni preached a sermon about "ministering to the stranger among us." For some moments that morning, there among us, he was "no longer a stranger."

Ray and Kay had invited Johnnie to stay at their home, and for a while he slept in the upper room of their barn. It was just before Christmas, and Detlef, one of the preachers on rotation, arranged for Johnnie to work in his office filling gift bags. Johnnie worked at the task with style and good humor for several days. During that time he even tolerated having his hair cut, taking a shower, and wearing traditional "office" clothes. Then one evening, he drove as usual back to Ray and Kay's home, went to bed, and in the morning, he was gone.

With his unpredictable appearances, and his vanishings, Johnnie was a constant reminder to us of the transient relationships in all our lives. However, most of the men who came to *La Sala* were much more constant in our region, rarely migrating from job to job following crops.

As friendships grew with the men, and as I became increasingly aware of their families and homes in Mexico, it seemed imperative that we establish a personal connection with those left behind south of the border in Oaxaca, Guanajuato, Michoacán, Guadalajara, Jalisco; and Mexico City. And so we decided to plan a trip.

11

Seeing Mexico for Myself

We must move away from asking God
to take care of the things that are
breaking our hearts
to praying about the things
that are breaking God's heart.

— Margaret Gibb
as quoted in *"Weekly Seeds"*
United Church of Christ

For several years I had been aware of a program called *VAMOS!*[14] created by Bill and Patty Coleman and Ike Patch in 1986. After a visit to Cuernavaca,[15] these three extraordinary people had become determined to improve the life of the very poorest Mexicans there. They were especially concerned for the welfare of children in urban centers. The *VAMOS!* centers not only provided nutrition and vitamins for these children, but they also trained local adults to become teachers in the schools.

One day I heard that a church group in our Northern California/Nevada UCC Conference was planning a trip to

---

[14] http://www.vamos.org.mx/
[15] in the state of Morelos, Mexico

Cuernavaca to see this program in action. They would stay with the Benedictine Sisters at the Guadalupe Center, and they would be taken to see firsthand how people survive in the dire circumstances there. Wanting to hear more details, I talked to Rev. Drew, a fellow pastor who led many of the Conference's immersion trips. He told me that those who had made this retreat came back filled with energy, and like brand new converts, they were ready to raise money for and offer their own energies to this extraordinarily effective mission. *Tenía ganas* (I felt the need) to go and see for myself, so I signed us up for the next tour.

In March 2004, Ellen and I packed our bags and left for a ten-day visit. On our way to Cuernavaca and the convent, our group stopped in Mexico City at the Benedictine Sisters' motherhouse. Here the sisters met our group of twenty and escorted us on a sightseeing trip around the city. We visited Tepeyac, the famous cathedral on the hill, and heard once again the story of *Nuestra Señora de Guadalupe* (Our Lady of Guadalupe).

Our guide also led us past the glass case where *la tilma* (the cloak) of Juan Diego rests, displaying the image of a crowned *Virgen* (Virgin) standing alone. We saw the larger-than-life statue of Juan Diego next to a bulletin board covered with "miracle pins." These pins, which include small representations of body parts—an arm, a leg, a heart—fastened to a crimson felt-covered board, represent the miraculous healings that have occurred in the lives of visitors. Stories handwritten on scraps of paper or on the backsides of envelopes, some including pictures, were also attached, all speaking of a deep gratitude to God. As I stood in the old cathedral, the mystery of God's presence caused my heart to pound and the blood to pulse noisily in my ears. Just two years earlier, Pope John Paul II had canonized Juan Diego, and the 400-year-old story of his meeting with Our Lady of Guadalupe seemed as fresh as today's news.

While we were in Mexico City, we saw the devastation caused by pollution there—particularly from gas-powered vehicles. And we heard about one way the government was trying to control that pollution: through an ordinance designed to reduce the number of vehicles on the streets. If the car or bus had a license number ending in an even number, it could be driven only on even days, and if the number ended in an odd number, it could only be used on odd-numbered days. Never could anyone choose to drive his or her car simply because it was convenient or needed because of a personal schedule. This meant that on the day our group went to Cuernavaca, only some were able to travel by convent van. The rest of us had to take public transportation—commuter trains and buses.

Once we arrived at the Guadalupe Retreat Center in Cuernavaca, each of us unloaded the medical, personal hygiene, and school supplies that we had stuffed into our second, allotted *maleta* (suitcase). We had been asked to bring that suitcase full of items to donate and we gathered school supplies along with personal care items and clothing to be left with the sisters there for distribution. Then we headed for the heart of the city, to the *Catedral* (Cathedral) and to *La Estación abandonada* (the abandoned train station) which had become home to thousands of displaced people. Shanty homes by the hundreds crowded around this station. It was a place where dozens of households sometimes plugged into the same electrical sources, where walls were often made of tin, where strikingly colorful birds and scrawny pets roamed *las calles* (the streets). But there were flowers growing out of every crack. And a few houses actually sported coats of *bien vivo* (brightly colored) stucco. We could see that some of the men were painting and expanding these improvised homes, probably getting ready to take in additional family members, providing a safe harbor for all.

When I asked the sisters at the convent why there were lots of people but no trains in the big, central station, they told me what had happened. It seems that many years ago *los ferrocarilles* (the trains) did run regularly between Mexico City and Huatulco on the Oaxacan coast. It was a commuter line, carrying people and goods between the Pacific Coast and the Capitol on a regular schedule. But around 1994, *el tren* (the train) ceased to operate. A Japanese company had purchased the cars from the train operator and shipped them elsewhere. The train simply ceased to exist.

Without the train, it became difficult for the moms and children to make the trips back to their villages to bring their farm goods and *artesanía* (handcrafted items) to market. Out of the same desperation that drove the men north to work in our fields, the women and children began to stay in the city, hunkering down in the marketplace or in the empty train station. Here, unfortunately, they had few resources, sanitary facilities or water; and without money for shoes, the children could not attend school. They began to re-sell what they could find in the public markets—*chicle*, (gum), *lápices* (pencils), and baubles.

Before we toured the area, the Benedictine Sisters in Cuernavaca offered us an immersion into the economics, legal issues, politics, church history and archaeological wonders of the state of Morelos. They introduced us to local experts and translated our dialogues with them, and then they took us to meet the families to whom they ministered in *La Estación*. The sisters helped organize Spanish-speaking *comunidades de base* (house churches) for these families in urban *barrios* (neighborhoods) who came together to worship and practice their faith in community.

The sisters also took us to see the community facilities of *VAMOS!*, the program of nurturing and nutrition for children I had wanted to see. A cornerstone of the *VAMOS!* program is the daily feeding and distribution of vitamin pills to kids. And along with this very practical activity, the adults are offered practice in community organizing, instruction in construction skills, and teacher training. The goal is to empower the adults to become more skilled and self-sufficient, and in the process some adults will have actually created a new community center, or learned how to teach basic skills to kids, or built new composting toilets for the center. Adults gain useful skills; kids grow healthier; and all know they are part of a community.

At the retreat center where we stayed, we had the option to attend masses morning and evening with the sisters. We enjoyed both silent meals and chattering meals, and took our turn at setting the table, serving, and cleaning up. We found ourselves able to hear, see, and taste the hospitality for which the Benedictines are known and which embodies our shared call to ministry.

During our first visit, we also met the ladies from the *La Nopalera* (a patch of prickly pear cactus) sewing cooperative. These women embroider T-shirts to sell to visitors, and this allows the co-op to be self-supporting. Other handmade items were also offered for sale, but the T-shirts captured our hearts and imagination. I asked how much the raw materials for the shirts cost and how much they charged for the shirts. They told me that $5 covered the raw materials, and they usually received $15 to $20 a shirt from visitors. Quickly I checked to see how much cash I had on me, and I made a donation for an assortment of thirty-five shirts to carry home. When I got home I asked for donations of $25 to $35 or more from people in the Bay Area, with the idea that we would return the entire amount to the women of *La Nopalera.*

Those first shirts sold so quickly to friends and church people during Winter Faire that I was able to send a healthy check back to the collective in the hands of another group of pilgrims to the Benedictine sisters. Along with that check, I sent an order for a second batch of shirts. Two pastors on that trip— one from the West Coast and the other from Florida— volunteered to shuttle those shirts back to the United States or to send them to us at their expense. What a kind connection that was, widening our circle of care even more than we could have imagined.

I was blessed to make this pilgrimage to Cuernavaca twice. As soon as we landed in Mexico City on that second trip, I ordered 100 shirts—a very large order for these hard-working women. They began sewing as soon as I placed the order, and they assured me the shirts would be ready by the time I left for home. Unfortunately, a few days later when I met with four of the ladies in Cuernavaca, it was clear just how tall an order this was.

The morning of that second departure, I had no shirts. Sadly, I surmised that the shirts I'd ordered would have to be delivered to Pescadero at a later date by other returning visitors. But as I stood in the doorway with my bags packed, waiting for our transportation, Yesenia jumped off the public bus and ran toward me, breathless to catch me before I left. She carried a white plastic tarp tied off with blue braided rope. It was a bundle full of *playeras* (T-shirts) still damp from their last washing (during which the women erase the patterns drawn on the fabric) and freshly ironed. The shirts were exquisite— embroidered in vibrant tones of *rojo, rosa, azul, blanco, amarillo, verde, morado y anaranjado* (red, pink, blue, white, yellow, green, purple and orange), each with its own unique, hand-worked *diseño* (design). Some featured the United Church of Christ slogan, *"Qué seamos uno"* ("That they may all be one") along with a circle of *niños* (children) with *manos* (hands) joined. Others featured the slogan, *"La tierra es de los quien la trabaja"* ("The land belongs to those who work it").[16] Still others sported *tortugas* (turtles) or *aves* (birds) or *mariposas* (butterflies) or traditional Mayan and Aztec designs. The shirts came in children's, women's, and even very large men's sizes. I filled my suitcase with them and carried them home to sell. We returned all the contributions for the shirts to the women in Mexico as our mission once again.

Finally we had created a bridge between Pescadero and Cuernavaca! Many of us proudly sported our bright, embroidered T-shirts as a symbol of that new connection. Wherever we took the shirts, people snapped them up, buying several for family members, for holiday gifts, or just to be part of the connection to Mexico. Nancy, one faithful volunteer from Butano Canyon who especially loved the shirts, bought at least a dozen as gifts for members of her extended family that first *Navidad* (Christmas)! She became a solid, life-long volunteer for

---

[16] by Emiliano Zapata (1879-1919) during the Mexican Revolution, 1910.

Puente, making a difference on both sides of the border. While she was not fluent in Spanish, she was present to our men no matter the language barrier—and she always had a welcoming smile.

The shirts also became part of my "show-and-tell kit" whenever I went to make a Puente presentation. Each shirt had its own card attached telling the story of the women in Mexico and their collective. And each served as a tangible reminder of those women left behind in Mexico, working with dignity to survive while their men labored in the north.

I have no idea how many hundreds of shirts have found their way into the lives of people connected to our Bay Area. Several of the church congregations that supported Puente during our early bike roundups pitched in to sell those shirts on behalf of the women they did not know. The Ladera UCC church bought $1,000 worth, opening the opportunity for their congregants to give them as gifts that year. Other people carried the love by covering the expenses for the women's collective—supplying them with enough money to weather sickness, loss of jobs, and natural disasters. For over a decade, these shirts served to stitch our hearts together across that infamous border.

One day an order of T-shirts arrived in my office with a letter enclosed. The letter, which was signed by each woman in the collective, expressed warm gratitude for the Puente Ministry. And it included a donation to Puente of several hundred dollars—still in Mexican pesos—wrapped in a special packet!

We exchanged the pesos at the bank and entered this gracious *don* (gift) into our records. We were neighbors, loving each other as we loved ourselves, and it was good.

12

Becoming a Compassionate Community

Be devoted to each other like a loving family.
Excel in showing honor and respect.

— Romans 12:10

As the seasons slipped by, more people joined in bridge-building. The town and its surrounding ranches became a community where newcomers who appeared did not remain strangers for long. And the men who had lived in the shadows for so long began to emerge and become an active part of our community. We celebrated together, worked together filling sandbags or sorting groceries, and learned *confiar* (to trust) each other. Included in this trust was respect and mutual acceptance; we had developed a caring for each other that marks families at their best. Now, townspeople could be heard shouting "*¡Hola, Gabi*" o "*Hola, Edi!*" ("Hi, Gabriel" or "Hi Edi!") Sometimes a joke would be shared, and laughter would follow. What a difference from my first days in Pescadero!

I became a daily presence in the lives of the men: for some I even became their confidante. New levels of *confianza* (trust) also developed among the brothers—precious connections that grew out of their time together at *La Sala*. Puente volunteers, too, experienced an increase in trust, and some of them invited the men into their homes for meals or arranged weekend jobs.

From our more intimate conversations, I began to develop a better sense of the challenges and difficulties that these men faced daily. Specifically, I learned that many of the men had little control over their working conditions. They were always at risk of being taken advantage of by employers. And I also came to understand that they took very poor care of their health.

One of those who faced significant health problems was Bartolomé. Over the course of several months, I bumped into Bartolomé in town. I could see that he was becoming more frail and exhausted every time I met him. One day *sus compañeros* (his buddies) told me that he could no longer get to work. When I heard that, I drove out to the ranch where he lived *para averiguarlo* (to see for myself). He did not look good. I persuaded him to come with me to the County Health Department Mobile Clinic where they examined him and took a blood test. They told us he was dangerously anemic and needed to change his diet.

Bartolomé wanted to improve his health so that he could return to work, but he had no intention of changing what he ate. The brothers encouraged him to put more than *papas y arroz* (potatoes and rice) and occasional *frijoles* (beans) in his burritos. I, on the other hand, ventured off to find him some iron supplements, along with *pasas, ensalada de espinaca para llevar, brócoli y verduras* (raisins, spinach salad to go, broccoli and green vegetables), a pound or two of *hamburguesa* (hamburger) and some other *carne de res* (beef)! He grudgingly sampled the foods I brought him, and slowly some of his vigor returned. I knew all too well that for these brothers *su propio nutrición y salud* (their own nutrition and health) was not the first order of business. Working in order to send money home to their wives, children, and wider families literally consumed them *día y noche* (day and night).

The struggle to maintain physical health was always a challenge for these men. But our most shocking loss came with

Mauricio's story. Mauricio, a dear friend and "regular," had been with us from the first days of our ministry. Always sporting a *gorro rojo* (red baseball cap), a leather *cinturón* (belt) on which was tooled the name of his home state, handmade and intricately adorned *botas de vaqueros* (cowboy boots), and that distinguished *bigote* (mustache), he would sit on the church steps and chat for hours. ¡*Qué guapo* (What a charmer)! This man *fue un artista con cuero* (was an artistic leather crafter). In Mexico he had earned his living making jackets, boots and belts; but, here he worked in *los invernaderos* (the greenhouses), tending the computerized climate control systems at night and delivering flowers to the wholesale flower market near Giants stadium in San Francisco in the early morning. Because of his work hours, he rarely had time to see his blood kin in the valley.

Mauricio knew all our volunteers, and he had mentored many of the younger men who came to the ranch where he lived and worked. It was he who convinced many of them to stop smoking and drinking as he had. And it was he who availed himself of the services of the local clinics in order to improve his general health.

Mauricio would often play his guitar and lead his buddies in song, with his powerfully compelling, scratchy former-smoker's voice. On the last day before the Thanksgiving feast at *La Sala*, he sang for hours, along with Gabriel, Luz and Santiago. One of them owned a tiny, wire-bound notebook with the titles of nearly *cien* (a hundred) of their old favorites, Mexican songs that had long grounded them and that expressed their emotions keenly. That notebook was like a *Biblia* (Bible) or a *himnario* (hymnal) to them, and they literally sang "every song in the book."

After that songfest, Mauricio went back to his ranch apartment—and I never saw him again. As the story was told to me: a few days after Thanksgiving, Mauricio's roommates heard a shot, ran into his room, and found him dead. One of them yelled, "*Mauricio fue matado!* (Mauricio has been shot!)" And that was the message that ricocheted off the hills, to the heartbreak of all who knew him. *¡No lo creía!* (Unbelievable!) None of us could accept the truth!

In the confusion of that day, *un chisme* (a rumor) ran rampant that Mauricio's best friend had fired the gun that killed him. When anyone called to offer condolences, that rumor was on their lips. Even his family in Mexico heard it. How could that be? And his best friend, bereft with his own grief, was stricken speechless. He knew it was not true. It was flat-out not true! I knew that it could not be true, too, for I had known both Mauricio and his friend for several years, talked many hours with both of them, and had experienced the depth of their friendship. This was not murder; clearly Mauricio had taken his own life. Patiently, I found myself explaining to anyone who called or approached me that day that Mauricio had indeed shot himself. Because these men had come to trust me, their disbelief finally faded, and they came reluctantly to accept the truth. Some apologized to Mauricio's friend for falsely accusing him. All of us grieved. Hard though it was to accept, we came to terms with the fact that Mauricio had taken his own life and was gone.

Later when I pondered the cause of his death with his family in Mexico, I made it very clear exactly what had happened. Puente's bridge carried the truth back to his family including his dad and grandparents, children at home. This salved the injury for his best friend who had been so falsely accused. These were very tender steps to bridge at this critical time.

We later found out that Mauricio had suffered numerous losses in recent years. Both his wife and baby had died in childbirth in Mexico, and he *había llevado su dolor* (had carried his grief) over those deaths as he made the trip north to work, never mentioning the pain to anyone here. Then his mother *se murió* (passed away), and he *no podía regresar* (was unable to return) to Mexico for the funeral: it was impossible for him *lamentarse con la familia* (to grieve with his family), *compartir* (to share in) the funeral arrangements, *celebrar su vida ni en el rosario ni la misa* (to celebrate her life at either the rosary or the mass), *ni de estar de luto* (or even to mourn) with his two other children. We had heard about his mother's death and we knew of his grief and anguish, but all we could do to mark her passing was to lower the Pescadero flag to *media hasta* (half mast). Still, *se rompió el corazón* (his heart was broken). To grieve his mother's loss alone may have been *demasiado* (too much).

Of course, we will never be sure exactly *que se rompió el espíritu* (what tore the life out of him) that Sunday morning. But Mauricio's death, in my mind, will always bear witness to *la soledad horrible* (the terrible loneliness) and the desperate homesickness *a dentro* (within) so many of The Men Alone.

Una misa (A mass) celebrating Mauricio's life was offered to a gathering of folks at St. Anthony's church. Looking around that day, I could see that the crowd filling the sanctuary and the balcony included both Spanish- and English-speaking people in about equal numbers. It was a community brought together—like so many families—out of tragedy. During the service, Father Medina addressed the issue of Mauricio's suicide with great care. He told the story of a French priest preparing a funeral mass for a young man who had jumped to his death off a bridge. Because the priest intended to hold mass for someone who *se suicidó* (had taken his own life), and because he planned to bury the young man's body within *los paredes y las fronteras* (the walls and borders) of the church cemetery, he was brought up before his superiors and threatened with being de-frocked. Undaunted, the priest went ahead with the mass, ending his homily with the simple statement, *"Entre el puente y el río este joven se reconcilió su vida con su Dios"* ("between the bridge and the river, this young man had made his life right with his God"). For this homily, he was exonerated.

In telling this story at Mauricio's funeral mass, Father Medina reminded us—in both English and Spanish—that death is to be honored, and that our faith congregations' and bi-cultural community's only need was to trust in God's unity and communion in life and death. It was a beautiful service.

After the mass, the community expressed its regard for Mauricio by setting out *una lata adornada con una fotografía de*

Mauricio (a can decorated with a photograph of Mauricio) at *Los Amigos taquería*, as was the tradition. Hundreds of dollars were gathered to help pay for his transportation home and his funeral arrangements there. *También el dueño y jefe mandó una donación* (What's more, his landlord, who was also his boss, sent money) to Mauricio's *abuelo* (grandpa) in Mexico to help support the children in Mauricio's family who were living with this grandfather.

Puente encouraged our county mental health worker, Mary Em, to offer one-on-one counseling to the young men on the ranch who had held Mauricio in such high esteem, looking up to him as a father-figure. And the owner of the ranch where Mauricio worked approached me and asked if I would *venir a ofrecer una bendición al cuarto* (come bless the room) where Mauricio had died so that his roommates could return to that room *en paz* (in peace). *Yo sintiendo tan honrada* (I felt so honored) to officiate at this rite!

Because Mauricio died of a gunshot wound, there was a sheriff's investigation. We spent days seeking out blood kin in the area who could identify Mauricio's *cuerpo* (body) and sign the release papers, and for this reason his body *no podía salir de Los Estados Unidos a Mexico hasta La Nochebuena* (could not be released to be sent to Mexico until Christmas Eve). Puente worked with the Mexican consulate to arrange the transport of his body at half the usual cost. Even so, the waiting time for a flight to carry a coffin to Mexico could be *meses* (months). *Fue un milagro* (it was a miracle) that a consulate official referred Puente to a mortuary in San Diego that agreed to receive his body *gratis* (free) and get it quickly on a flight home.

The family was greatly relieved. Not only would Mauricio's body soon arrive home in Guadalajara, but they were also freed of the $80-per-day fee that the San Mateo County morgue had been charging to keep the body for the past several weeks. Finally, Mauricio's dear friend, who had been *acusado aunque era falso* (wrongly accused), came forward to say that his family lived in the same area of Mexico and operated *un funerario* (a mortuary). The family, he said, would provide the final services for Mauricio.

The regular turning of the seasons—from life to death to life again—was surely palpable in that terrible year. I carried my grief as if Mauricio had been a part of my own birth family.

Some of our work on behalf of the men had a better outcome. One day as I was visiting one of the outlying farms, I was approached by Ramón, who asked quietly if I could help his crew get paid *las pagas* (the wages) they had been promised. Valentino, Alberto, Cristiano, Carlos, Antonio, Primitivo, Arturo, Rudolfo, and Martín—none of them had received full wages for several years. Each man—and his family, if they were with him—had been provided with *una vivienda* (a place to stay) and a $100 monthly stipend for food, but most of them were owed substantial additional wages—*miles de dólares* (thousands of dollars), in some cases. Clearly, Ramón was another brother who had come to trust Puente.

I told him I would need to gather all the facts and then see what could be done. Most of The Men Alone worked for people who treated them fairly; I could only hope that this situation was the exception. The following week, I invited the workers from that farm to come to *La Sala* and to bring with them any notes they had about wages due. When I got back to my home office, I called Mike at California Rural Legal Assistance in Watsonville and explained the situation. He promised to send someone out to *La Sala, para escuchar y pedir justicia* (to listen and to seek justice) for these men, our brothers.

The following Thursday evening, Daniela—a representative from California Rural Legal Assistance—and I sat down with Ramón, who was owed the largest amount, and recorded his story. He knew the crops he had worked each day—*cebolla, esprado, guisantes* (onions, Brussels sprouts, peas), and the amount of back wages he was owed for that work. Every day he had tallied his hours in a tiny, well-worn, lined, daily journal, which was the same kind of notebook that many of us used in our college studies. Once Ramón had finished documenting his claim, nine other workers laid out the details of their claims. Daniela carried all this information back to her office. She later called me to say that she intended to file a claim on the men's behalf. This California Rural Legal Assistance representative was yet another voice for the voiceless!

As this story unfolded, I sought out the rancher who had hired the men. He was *en bancarrota* (in bankruptcy): literally, *no tenía ni dinero para pagarles* (he had no money to pay his workers). In fact, he was so far in the hole that he had not even mentioned *estos sueldos ni estas deudas* (these salaries or debts) in his bankruptcy filing. I warned him that his delinquency in paying his workers had been documented and that California Rural Legal Assistance would be filing a claim. And I asked him if he wanted to talk about how he could pay the men.

He was not willing to meet me at my home on the main street since it was *tan visible* (fully visible) to the community passing by. But he said he would meet me at his home. We were able to develop a relatively cordial *amistad* (relationship), in part because I knew his family—mother, father and brothers. Through negotiation, we came to an agreement, and *un abogado* (an attorney) was able to arrange a partial payment for each of the men. Unfortunately, the payment was only pennies on the dollar. And because claims on unpaid wages are only valid for one year (some of these claims were four years old), many of the claims were simply written off as "lost wages." This was one of only two labor confrontations we faced in my ten years of ministry.

It was a temptation to take the local newspaper reporter out to the ranch to take pictures and write up a story. However, I had made a commitment to all the ranch owners when I first asked to visit the men who lived on their properties that I would never bring anyone else without their permission. But the men themselves were quite free to talk to a reporter or to invite a news photographer to take photos of their living spaces, and Valentino decided to speak to the newspaper. He met with a reporter *al correo* (at the post office) and later took him to the ranch to get pictures. When the article appeared in the local paper, it was clear to me that the workers had found their own voice and could stand their ground. Of course, I was immediately drawn into a community discussion of these events.

For the most part, our ranchers were hard-working people with problems of their own. *Se hace muy dificil sobrevivir si uno es dueño del rancho también* (it is also hard for small farmers to survive), and to pay their production costs for seed, set plants, equipment, fertilizers, labor and transportation. Markets change, weather ruins planting, products priced *más barato* (cheaper) undercut the market. Harder still, growers from other countries sometimes price their produce below the subsistence levels of growers in this country.

Moreover, many of our community growers and farmers were approaching retirement age and were no longer able to labor as intensively as they once did. And sons and daughters had often found jobs out of town. There seemed to be no "next generation" to take over the farms.

Workers who were not employed on ranches or farms often found work at the local mushroom factory. Golden Mushrooms, originally Campbell's Mushrooms, offered some of the best paying jobs in the area: hourly rates at that time were $10 plus bonuses; and compensation also included health, dental and vision benefits with *una enfermera* (a nurse) on site. But the factory had no on-site housing, and so the men who worked there had to commute twenty miles *ida y vuelta* (round trip)—illegally, of course. (Nearly half the workers at the mushroom factory lived in Santa Cruz—and commuted forty miles round trip.) Workers signed up for any of three shifts and made that drive every day. I'd hoped that they would simply share rides, but that was not the custom. Usually riders would pay a fee to ride with whoever had a car.

Transportation was only one of the problems associated with working at the mushroom factory. *El moho* (the mold) in the *hongueras* (mushroom houses) was hard on *los pulmones de los trabajaderos* (the workers' lungs). What's more, during my tenure, Golden Mushrooms closed and re-opened three times; and each time it re-opened, it was operated by a different corporation. I later discovered that these closures were due to the fact that mushroom houses need to lie fallow every third year. It is hard to imagine the toll and strain on workers who are laid off every three years and who might have to wait out a year to see who would be rehired by new management.

One day news came that the mushroom factory would close for good at the end of *la quincena* (the two-week) pay period. After filing for bankruptcy, the Canadian owners had simply shut down all their US plants. Now I knew there would be 350 workers suddenly *sin trabajo* (without work), about half of whom lived in and around Pescadero.

Not long after that, we found out that the Eastside ranch was closing. The day I found out, I raced out to the ranch to see for myself. The workers told me, "*¡Tenemos que irnos el 30 de mayo* (we have to be out May 30)!" The owner had borrowed often trying to keep the ranch going, but he could no longer meet his loan payments; his only alternative was to declare bankruptcy. Not only was the ranch to be closed, but all the on-site housing was to be lost, too.

The timing of this second closure and eviction was particularly devastating. The children were in school until mid-June, after which many of them were enrolled in summer school camps, which were important for the well-being of the children.

Los dos agencias (the two agencies) North Street and Puente clearly needed to take action. Several of the workers with children in school set up a meeting with the land owners—and a few townspeople joined them—to ask for an extension of the eviction date until the end of summer. This seemed a reasonable request for the sake of the children, and it was accepted.

Then the hard work began. Over the next several weeks, both agencies worked to relocate those who had been laid off either by the mushroom factory or by the Eastside ranch. These were friends, and friends of friends, and we wanted to do everything we could to help them through this painful time. Using money from a special grant, we rented a year's worth of storage space in Half Moon Bay; and within days, with the help of Catholic Worker friends Mike and Kathy, we began to trek the workers' appliances and large furniture to the storage facility, since they could not transport these things in cars, on bikes, or on foot themselves. Ironically, during the previous year, many workers had qualified for a Community Action Agency grant arranged by Socorro, the high school's administrative assistant, in collaboration with the Farm Bureau. This grant had provided the workers with energy-efficient refrigerators, light bulbs, and microwave ovens. Now, how could the brothers and families move all this stuff? What else could we do but shuttle and store these new appliances—and the rest of their life's possessions—while they looked for new homes?

We found that as soon as the church folks heard about the situation, groceries and meals—fruit, juice, rice and beans— began to flow in. It was *muy triste y muy rico a la vez* (both a very sad and a very rich time). But where would the displaced families live? Rental housing in Pescadero is both *caro* (costly) and in short supply. If a working family were lucky enough to find a rental unit in town, the cost of rent would require that at least one adult have a full time job. For this reason, the displaced people could not simply move into the village of Pescadero.

And going to *la ciudad* (the city) of Half Moon Bay, a much larger town, was a culture shock indeed. Nonetheless, many of the displaced people did move in with family and friends in Half Moon Bay, and some of them commuted down the coast each day so that they could maintain their jobs and their children could go to school in Pescadero. This produced additional gas costs, and, of course, driver's license issues. Other families pulled up roots entirely: our school district lost ten percent of its students during this time, a harsh blow for a tiny, rural district.

The owner of the Eastside ranch did not force the workers out or lock *su portón* (his gate) when the negotiated time was up. I happen to know that he quietly and graciously let some of the men stay in the horse barn through late fall. It was hard for him to see them all out of work and hurting.

While Eastside was in the process of shutting down, I stopped by for *la última visita* (one last visit) with the families there. On this ranch, the main barracks served as a community space, with *dos regaderas* (two showers) and *una cocina* (a kitchen), which had often been the site of shared meals with the men and their families when we delivered food or holiday treats. There was a small altar in that space which usually held *un bonche de flores en el jarrón* (a vase full of flowers). On the day of my last visit, while the men were all packing, I noticed that the flowers on the altar were gone, but a photo of *La Virgen de Guadalupe* (The Virgin of Guadalupe) was still on the wall.

"*No se olviden de Guadalupe* (don't forget Guadalupe)," I reminded them.

"*Tenga, usted* (take her)," one of the men replied.

I hardly knew what to say. Beneath the picture was the phrase *Ruega Señora por Nosotros* (pray for us, Señora Guadalupe)—and yet, surprisingly, the men had decided to leave her behind. Perhaps I would never know why. *Yo me dió cuenta inmediatemente* (suddenly I realized) that this was not the time to ask for explanations. She was a gift offered to me—a gift to be graciously received. *Trato hecho* (that was how it needed to be done). So without discerning further, I carefully peeled the tape off the wall. This picture found a very special place high above the other pictures on the wall in our Puente office. And she continues to have a place in our home where we can see her each morning. Guadalupe is the spirit that sustains hope for us all *ayer, hoy y para siempre* (yesterday, today, and forever).

As if the closure of the big mushroom plant and the bankruptcy at the Eastside ranch weren't enough, in late autumn we learned that the other *honguerita* (little mushroom farm) south of town at Pigeon Point was to close immediately— and its workers were to be evicted. Now there would be ten more families to relocate—a total of nearly forty men, women and children with no place to live and no jobs. This third closure came because the County Environmental Health Department had red-tagged the housing at the mushroom farm. The housing manager had apparently *no había arreglado* (not made the repairs) specified in several earlier inspections, and now the housing was deemed unfit for human habitation. And this had triggered the business' demise.

Driving that day to the farm, I stopped the car at one of the coastal highway viewpoints. I took some deep breaths and focused on the vibrant colors of late fall crops draping the hills. Slowly, I rotated my gaze until it rested finally on the sparkling waters of the Pacific. The waves continued beating their rhythmic melody against the rocks below. Here spread for me in a 360-degree panorama was a dazzling reminder of God's gracious presence even on a day when another major displacement was about to begin.

As I approached the camp, I saw several buildings used as housing by worker families. Bright Christmas lights and decorations were strung about, the only signs of comfort and joy, as *La Navidad* (Christmas) approached. The irony was that though this made the season bearable, the electrical display contributed to these families' perilous living situation. The A-frame on the property had *paredes de cartones* (cardboard interior walls) with little window openings between each "room." The flimsy barriers created four dark living spaces, which were home to several families. The two-car garage also had temporary walls that created four small *habitaciones* (apartments), each housing a family of three or four. The garage was "wired" with extension cords hanging from the cardboard dividers, an inferno waiting to happen.

I could see raw sewage running from the overcrowded A-frame house across the ground to the greenhouses, trailers, and garages where other workers lived. Some of the plastic-covered Quonset huts which had been used as mushroom greenhouses had been converted to barracks where the young men, recent arrivals, would sleep. The smell, the mold, the damp coastal night air, and the steam from the day's sun would make these abodes repulsive—and dangerously unhealthy for any human being. This was something I had not seen before— and it was very painful to take in. I remembered that in years past when we had delivered Second Harvest leftovers to this compound, we had always passed the food under *la cerca del alambre de púas* (the barbed wire fence) at the locked gate. Now I knew why.

On that difficult day, I met with the workers and listened to their frantic stories. I was told that some weeks earlier, *los oficiales de los bomberos* (the fire department officers) had come to inspect the property and to see if the manager had made the required *mejoramientos* (improvements). The officials came in uniform, accompanied by a sheriff's car. There happened to be ten young, single men, recently arrived, living in the abandoned mushroom greenhouses. And when they saw the "men in uniform," they started running—and were never seen again.

I also heard from the workers that they wanted to pay *su renta* (their rent) even though the place was deemed unfit for human habitation; they seemed to feel they had no place to go. These families clearly had lived in terror for a long time, having been threatened with stories of deportation by *La Migra* (INS—now called ICE). I tried to convince them that they would find another place to live somewhere, and that it was not necessary to pay more rent when the owner had not made the place safe to inhabit. In fact, the owner could not legally ask for rent.

El dueño (the owner) of the farm had never been seen in the area; and so, on that day, I sought out the manager. He spoke Tagalog and very little Spanish, which made it difficult for the workers to trust him, and he seemed arrogant to me. The women who lived there had told me that the manager had repeatedly intruded on the families, claiming he was visiting on behalf of the owner; and at one point, he had allegedly demanded that the families loan him money for a car, threatening to throw them out if they did not comply. And now the manager had refused to make the required repairs on the farm. His unwillingness to see the dangers in the living conditions of the workers, their families and children, and his blatant unwillingness to clean up the property was about to render them all homeless.

Puente later interceded with the County in this case, crafting what we hoped were clear and compassionate arguments for the environmental health officers, and pleading for a month's extension on the eviction. They understood, and allowed the workers and their families additional time to find new housing. When a community has built bonds of trust and caring, even disasters such as these become more manageable.

In the face of all these housing and job losses, we began to receive some blessings. First, we were offered some emergency housing funds from San Mateo County housing program, which we used to pay rental deposits for several families. Then, through the Philanthropic Ventures Foundation, we received a grant to provide meal coupons for those people being relocated. And all along, individuals made small donations designated for those caught in this misery.

"Make a new field in the donor database," I told Margaret, as I tossed a handful of envelopes onto her desk one day, "and call it 'Relocation.' The Half Moon Bay paper just ran a powerful article describing the closures and the families who have to find a new place to live. ¡*Mira* (and just look)! People are sending in checks, offering to help!" Indeed, that day I had delivered to Margaret several hundred dollars worth of checks ready to be entered and deposited. And this was just a beginning. Before the crisis ended, a substantial amount flowed in to assist families with their moves. The whole local community rallied to help.

A few weeks later I drove past the place where the little mushroom farm had been. I was astonished at the transformation! The old, tattered, plastic-covered greenhouses had been torn down, and all the buildings had been freshly painted, in bright barn-red with sparkling-white trim. There were even newly constructed, white picket fences. A large *Se Vende* (For Sale) sign posted on one of the fences offered the property at over a million dollars.

It was as if the old housing had never existed! Much like the World War II Japanese internment camp in Bean Hollow just down the road, nothing remained from this sad and painful chapter. All the traveler now sees is a nicely painted ranch house surrounded by lush property.

On my last visit to that site, I felt as though I ought to build *un altar* (an altar), as is customary in Mexican culture, to mark the losses that its small community of workers had suffered. In the end, our friends dispersed to live with family members in the area, or relocated to other communities, all in the hope of finding new jobs before the roughest of winter weather set in.

In sharp contrast to such unsanitary and unsavory sites, other growers and ranchers in the area offered quite comfortable worker housing. Several of the growers told me they felt that adequate housing was very important in attracting and keeping responsible workers. The local rancher who produced gourmet-quality goat cheese, was particularly attuned to the needs of the workers. She had honed her Spanish in a language and culture immersion program in Central America. She always noticed the newly-arrived family members of any of the workers she employed; and as she was able, she would offer these family members first choice of any jobs she might have on the ranch. When she heard of the ordeal at the mushroom factory, she ordered a large modular home, which she then rented to several of the displaced families.

Another local nursery provided much-needed family and singles housing for many years. The owner had constructed cement block structures and rented them at very nominal rates. And the owners of a local organic farm also worked over the years to alleviate the workers' housing plight. Decades ago, they had built a brick house with passive solar heating on the property to live in. When they hired their first five workers to work their fields, they built a second house just like the first one to be shared by those five single men. And when one of the workers later asked to bring his family from Mexico, they built yet another home for that family. This happened again and again, until five workers' dwellings sat beside the owner's home circling the edge of the fragrant herb gardens.

Not only did some of the growers provide safe, appropriate housing for their workers, but they also invited the San Mateo County Health Services van to stop on their properties to serve the workers. The van would begin its circuit by visiting a ranch near Año Nuevo Elephant Seal Reserve at the southern border of the county, nearly twenty miles from town. It would come north, visiting three other nurseries and ranches before reaching town where the ranchers across from the schools allowed it to park at lunchtime. We all had the same goals: to help maintain the health of workers and their families, who would then help sustain the local economy and well-being of all.

The County Health Department's medical staff had been visiting Pescadero for some twenty years—ever since Clara, the wife of our senior pastor, Rev. Orril, and several other women had established a well-baby clinic in town. In 1996, the well-baby clinic was replaced by a mobile van which continued to provide well-baby care, plus family planning and—because the closest doctors were located in Half Moon Bay, San Mateo or Santa Cruz—a variety of other services. The regular van staff became known and trusted in town, partly because they were connected to my partner, Ellen. Word spread as far as Mexico that Pescadero was a safe place to live, a place where one could have access to adequate healthcare services, and that "Wendy was the '*Madre de Pescadero*' ('Mother of Pescadero')."

With local media coverage of the closures and our relocation efforts, many more people in the Bay Area learned about the Puente Ministry out in Pescadero. The *Half Moon Bay Review, San Mateo Times, San Francisco Chronicle* and *San Jose Mercury News* all ran articles about our work. *Univision* television, Channel 14, also covered many Puente activities. Suddenly, it was not just the United Church of Christ congregations that got it. Folks from up and down the Peninsula booked tours, county officials visited, and people who had never paid much attention to the southwest corner of San Mateo County began to recognize that something was happening.

When we first came to Pescadero, we thought that the South Coast region would always be invisible, underserved, and isolated; we had represented ourselves as such in all of our grant applications and presentations. But this was no longer true!

It was not long after this tumultuous period that I realized we hadn't seen Johnnie Angel in months. I couldn't help but wonder how he was faring out there on the road—and whether he had fallen ill somewhere. He never looked particularly healthy, we didn't know how old he was, and he certainly lived a hazardous existence.

Then one day our intern, Moni, received a phone call. The voice on the other end told her that Johnnie had died on the streets in Arizona. And the only clue as to who might have an interest in his death was a business card in his pocket. Moni had given him that card the last time he was in Pescadero.

Ouzel, a friend from the Pescadero church, drove to Arizona to pick up Johnnie's body and return him to Pescadero. His memorial was held in the church, and several of his friends carried his coffin to the cemetery following the service. He lies there now, home at last.

13

Sustaining Our Mission

They asked only one thing,
that we remember the poor
which was actually what I was eager to do.

— Galatians 2:10

Now that our dream of a bridge between the Spanish-speaking and English-speaking folks in Pescadero was a functioning reality, how could we ensure that this bridge would remain viable into the future?

Our bridge felt quite solid to me, anchored at one end by the continuing enthusiasm of our church, of various faith groups around the Bay Area, and of the Pescadero community; and on the other end, by the workers themselves. Some of those men were the very same brothers I had met in the streets when I first arrived in town. Others came from the pool of new workers who were arriving at the rate of about seventy each year. People moved comfortably over our *puente* (bridge), which connected community resources to everyone who needed them.

But all of the visible activity that took place at the church, the Native Sons' Hall, neighbors' homes and ranches was underpinned by long hours of serious, thoughtful, and less visible administrative work.

While I worked from an office situated in the second bedroom of our home, Margaret handled much of the paperwork from her desk over the hill in San Mateo. Here she drafted grant proposals, filed grant reports, and investigated other sources of funding. We kept in constant contact via email and phone. And every Wednesday, we had lunch together and then sat side by side in her office, going over financial reports, drafting newsletters, and discussing the countless other details involved in the day-to-day operation of a growing ministry.

Reports on the financial status of our nonprofit were assembled for every meeting of our advisory committee. We agreed early on that we would offer complete transparency: every committee member would know every detail of the ministry. This careful reporting allowed our advisors to make responsible decisions as Puente's Ministry expanded. The original five-member advisory committee gradually grew; and when it became ten, we began to think of it as a possible Board of Directors.

In addition to our seed-money grant and the continuing support from the Pescadero church, we received grants from the Peninsula Community Foundation, the San Francisco Foundation, and Philanthropic Ventures Foundation. The United Church of Christ Northern California/Nevada Conference contributed "peace and justice" grants each year, and our former congregation in Belmont included Puente in its regular mission-giving, as did the Berkeley church and dozens of others. Modest individual donations were growing, too. These individual and church gifts comprised about half of the income that sustained our ministry from the beginning. As people learned about what Puente was doing, they wanted to be a part of it.

Whenever we took stock of the money situation, Margaret insisted that we keep careful records of every dollar we received and paid out. Weekly, I reviewed the total funds coming in, grateful for our blessings, joyfully acknowledging the existing resources we had, and making breathtaking plans for potential new funds. We worked diligently and faithfully to maintain enough reserve at the end of each year to fund obligations for the upcoming six months. Our guiding principle was to ensure the continuation of services for the men while we raised additional money.

The grants we received from the local foundations were set up on a three-year cycle: we were provided with a substantial amount each year for three consecutive years, and in the fourth year we were expected to cover expenses from other sources. We might, however, apply again in the fifth year. In each of the three years when we received funds, we were obligated to file a report of our activities detailing how we used the grant money; and we had to submit an application for the next year's grant. Program officers from these foundations would come to visit us before approving a grant, and often again as renewal time came around. Having had very limited experience with the grant process, I missed applying for the second year of one of those three-year grants, thinking that we should not ask again as Puente had enough money in the bank and did not need it! Imagine the foundation's surprise.

But in the end we did learn the process, and grant applications became easier. The standard questions all grantors asked were covered in our "boiler plate" and ready for the next opportunity. How grateful I was that Margaret assisted in the writing of these grant applications and reports. She also continued to handle the preparation and administration of our growing budget.

As I began to know the men better, I wanted the "regulars" to have an idea of how we were able to open *La Sala*, and how we could provide bikes, blankets, and beans. And so when I received the second year's invitation to attend a foundation award dinner, I decided to invite two or three of the men to attend with me.

That first time I took Mauricio and Gabriel with me. Since there was no one translating the proceedings into Spanish, I translated all evening, although I could see it was a bit distracting to the English-speaking attendees. The following year when other grantees began to attend with their "stakeholders," the foundation staff gladly provided Spanish translators, and the event became a more intimate and just gathering.

Over the years we got to know our program officers very well. Their advice and good counsel was so very helpful. We found that, with their aid, we became known as *un modelo* (a model) ministry for both the San Francisco Foundation and the Peninsula Community Foundation. Designated donors who were particularly interested in migrant workers often visited our facilities to get a reality check regarding the agricultural world surrounding Pescadero. They would talk to the brothers and tour their work sites and living areas. Eyes were rarely dry on those trips, as some of these now-wealthy men and women donors were reminded of their own childhood experiences living around migrant workers in rural communities or on working farms. These person-to-person contacts were much more descriptive of our work than any grant application could ever be.

Our funding base grew to include more than fifteen significant granting sources. And as our funding increased, the salary available to me grew with the blessing of the advisory committee. Margaret began to receive some pay, too. Over the next several years, we worked to make these compensation packages comparable to other nonprofit organizations in the region. We knew that we would need to offer salaries that would attract replacements if either of us were unable to serve. As we laid these plans, there was little doubt that we were moving toward becoming a truly sustainable faith-based, nonprofit organization.

Foundations, in order to fully document their grants, need statistics. Our grantors usually asked how many people we served and in what ways. We really needed to keep track of those numbers, but how could we do that? We were temporarily stumped; the task seemed beyond our grasp. Then notice of a grant appeared from an agency made up of out-of-work Silicon Valley programmers who were willing to design an application for a local nonprofit *gratis* (without cost). We applied, and they accepted our application! Maybe *they* could create a record-keeping system that would meet our grantors' needs.

When they invited us to meet with them to discuss our needs, Margaret and I took the Bay Area Rapid Transit (commonly called "BART") to San Francisco and walked to their Union Square office. As we climbed the narrow stairs to their loft, we tried to gather our thoughts, but nothing could have prepared us for their barrage of questions. There were so many things to consider when building a custom database, particularly one that would track the kinds of services Puente provided to each and every person we encountered! Fortunately, our years of experience with our own donor database gave us a frame of reference for their questions. At least Margaret understood how databases worked!

In the end, it took over six months of weekly meetings to complete the project. Mostly it was just me taking BART to an office near the Giants' baseball stadium on the San Francisco Bay and fielding questions from the team assigned to our project. The database would be built using Access, a different software program from our donor database, and quite unfamiliar to me. While the information we would collect was important to our grantors, I lived in terror that immigration officials from the government might raid our office, take our database, and go after our men! I imagined tossing our computers into the surf before allowing those dear lives to be endangered.

Eventually, the database took shape and came to life in our offices. We gathered the names of over 500 men in that database and detailed how we served each one.

I continued to meet regularly with the advisory committee and as the number of men we served grew, we agreed that it was time to have their voices represented on this Committee. We asked two of our *trabajadores* (worker brothers) to join us, and we began holding all our deliberations in both English and Spanish. *Los Gabrieles* (The two: Gabriel, the elder; and Gabriel "Gabi," the younger) represented the voices of the men, keeping our service mission-based and moving in the direction of our call. As these two men became our friends, they called from our hearts a great deal of love which then kindled the potential for still more hospitality. Their presence also prompted us to turn our meetings into meals—*¡Cómo no!* (Of course!) How could we not break bread together and give thanks for all that had been given to Pescadero? *¡Todos los dones de Dios!* (All this has been a gift from God!)

To me, our bridge felt strong and sturdy; but there was always the question of its future. As Dick, our program officer at one community foundation, pointed out, "If anything were to happen to you or Ray or any of the other key people, would Puente collapse and be lost?" I vowed that we could not let that happen.

I began sharing with our advisory committee my concerns about ensuring that our ministry continue into the future. And I called on them to consider what steps needed to be taken to promote Puente as an independent nonprofit organization.

Fortunately, Peninsula Community Foundation offered technical support to its grantees, and it was from that organization that I arranged to have a consultant meet with our advisory committee to provide us with some general information about the process of becoming a nonprofit. Regina arrived, with her six-year-old in tow, on *el día de las madres* (Mother's Day) to join our regular advisory committee meeting. She brought to the meeting her extensive experience in guiding small faith-based start-ups through the often-difficult transformation from an ad hoc "mom-and-pop ministry" into a solid, functioning organization. As her little boy Matthew magically entertained himself with his toys, she held us in rapt attention. When she left we gathered up the handouts she'd provided and agreed to read them carefully, to think about all she'd told us, and to talk more about what our next steps might be.

The growing responsibilities of running Puente took most of my attention over the ensuing months, and we made no further decisions on this issue for about a year. Finally, the matter came up again at an advisory committee meeting, and we called in another consultant, this time to get serious about what steps might be taken in the process of becoming that nonprofit.

Our encounter with the next consultant was very different. Chuck, recently elected president of our group, had opened his *casa amplia en el campo* (spacious hilltop home) for our first-ever retreat. The purpose of that meeting was to decide, after a year's discernment, whether to apply for nonprofit status. We talked about our own *ganas, esperanzas y razones* (desires, hopes, and reasons) for supporting Puente's call, our own experiences as our *puente* (bridge) was being built, and the steps we thought we might take to stabilize the structure and make it strong enough to survive a change in leadership. When this second consultant began to make her presentation, we saw immediately that we were not prepared for such a different style of organization. We listened to horrifying descriptions of all we would need to go through to become a full-fledged nonprofit organization. She painted a picture that included very large budgets; a multi-person professional staff; specific fiscal and legal responsibilities for each committee member; and major, ongoing fundraising campaigns. She also told us firmly that we would have to split off from the church and become a free-standing agency—a "big business"!

The advisory committee blanched. They almost rose up and tossed her out. This was not the future we wanted for Puente. We were about relationships, not corporation-ship! It was too much for us to handle—and we tabled it.

However, we did agree to look ahead to a time when I would retire and someone else would head up the organization.

I did not yet want to consider a future in which I wasn't involved with Puente! This was what I was called to do, what I had unknowingly prepared for all my life. How could I possibly think of leaving it? Yet, how could I *not* prepare the way, knowing that day would come?

As part of the process of preparing for the future, we put out a call for new committee members. People began to appear, some making a commitment to stick with us just through the process of becoming a nonprofit, others signing on for a full three-year rotation. At the same time, several of our current board members rotated off the board. Slowly, a new group of people came together and began to coalesce into a fledgling Board of Directors.

Gracias a Dios (thanks be to God), Regina was willing to return to Puente and walk with us as we revisited the idea of becoming an official 501(c)(3) nonprofit organization. She walked us through the legal and tax implications, the planning that would need to be undertaken, and the commitment such a process would require. Her style and experience were like balm for *nuestros heridas* (our wounds) and served to stabilize our fearful hearts. In the end, we decided to go for it.

Chuck, who had become our board chair, took the lead in assembling the required materials for our application. During the process, he had to go online and find a domain name that was not already taken by another organization in either this country or Mexico. This task took days—and a dance at the computer that this pastor could hardly fathom. Finally, we settled on a new name: *Puente de la Costa Sur* (Bridge of the South Coast). It would have been grammatically more correct to be *Puente de la Costa del Sur*, but I chose what my colloquial street language experience brought to my heart —proving that I will be a Spanish-as-a-Second-Language student to my dying day! We registered our new domain name, and the plans for a website began spinning. Carol and Julia, both of whom understood the process of applying for nonprofit status because they were directors of other nonprofit agencies in the area, worked eagerly and efficiently on our behalf.

In May of 2004, Chuck submitted our application to the IRS. The IRS processing office was badly backlogged and understaffed, and so we waited. During the next several months, we took turns calling the IRS hotline to see if our paperwork had moved up the queue, all the while wondering if we'd submitted the right stuff. Finally, in December 2004, we received notice: the application had been approved! Puente was now officially Puente de la Costa Sur, a 501(c)(3) faith-based nonprofit corporation. ¡*Increíble* (incredible)!

While Chuck and others were applying for our nonprofit status, I was worrying about how we might find more suitable space for our new agency. I met with Carol from North Street Family Resource Center and Judy from South Coast Children's Services to see if we could find a site in town that the three agencies might share. I talked to the people who managed Native Sons' Hall, and looked at two adjoining apartments over the old thrift shop. The manager of those apartments turned us down because we worked with "those people." I heard that the high school expected to receive funding to build a community service wing, but when I investigated further, it turned out that the plan was still in the talking stage. I peeked and poked at every building in town, but there seemed to be no rooms available anywhere.

Finally, I discovered a building that appeared to be vacant and for sale—and it was right across the street from *La Sala*. I found out who the owner was, and realized that I had a speaking relationship with his son. One day I asked if I might talk with him about the property he had for sale. At his ranch over a piece of pumpkin pie at his invitation, we discussed the property. And when we parted, we both felt it might be possible to put together a deal in which the three service agencies would rent the whole building and divide up the available space among the organizations.

Armed with this very tentative rental agreement, several of us from these three agencies went to the Tides Foundation at the Presidio in San Francisco and described our dream of relocating together into one property. We had cooperated with the Tides Foundation on a number of events over the years, and I hoped that our request for support from that foundation would bear fruit. But it was not to be. The Tides representatives felt that we three agencies had not yet done the proper legwork nor agreed on a substantial-enough plan to become a "one-stop shopping" outfit.

At that point we dropped the idea of a joint facility, and I continued to look for a site for Puente alone. During those months, I often shared my longstanding *sueño* (dream) with the men: *¿Qué pasaría si la casa frente a mi casa pueda convertirse a nuestro hogar* (what if that house across the street from *La Sala* could be our new home)?

One day we noticed that the For Sale sign on this property had disappeared. We were crushed! Someone had purchased the building! But in fact, the new owner turned out to be our first advisory committee president, Jill. Since she was no longer involved with the day-to-day activities of Puente and worked "over the hill," her purchase took us all by surprise.

Then Jill told us the good news: she had decided to use one half of the single story addition for her own business office; the other half she offered to rent to Puente. The Board wasted no time in accepting!

This property consisted of a small single story addition that had been a restaurant in the front, and a three-bedroom house at the back. Jill completely rebuilt the commercial space. She sheet-rocked and painted the walls, stained and sealed the well-worn concrete floor, and installed new knobs, locks, and a door. When it was finished, our section consisted of a large *salón* (room), about twenty feet wide and twelve feet deep; a washroom with toilet and sink with cold-running water; and a small amount of storage. Windows filled the wall facing the street, letting in plenty of light and making our presence visible to passersby.

During the years when Puente's "office" was in my home, it had completely overtaken our second bedroom. And the rest of the Puente office stuff was still in the back room of Margaret's shop in San Mateo—space she had graciously donated for years. I was excited by the prospect of consolidating our offices and establishing Puente's roots in a single location on the Coast.

By that time, Margaret was ready to retire, having recently become *una abuela* (a grandmother), and so we began preparations to hire an administrative assistant. It was hard for me to imagine finding someone who could fill Margaret's shoes: she handled so many tasks, all of them important—and the two of us had been such a well-functioning team for so many years. Nonetheless, we developed a job description and posted the new position for "fund developer/office manager." Then we realized that Puente would also need a community outreach worker, or "COW," as we fondly dubbed the position, to work alongside me as executive director. It was difficult to parse out what I would focus on, what the new office staffer would do, and who would serve the men. As we assigned responsibilities to these job descriptions, I realized that there were many tasks involving The Men Alone that I would have to give up—tasks that I loved. I became overwhelmed by a sense of personal loss and sadness.

But the upside was that Puente would be an official organization with physical space and a staff! We posted the fund developer/office manager position in the fall of 2004, and the community outreach worker position in the spring of 2005. Both jobs were part time; but because we felt a strong obligation to act with integrity, and because we valued equality, we arranged for both positions to include salaries comparable to what other organizations paid for similar work, and full benefits beyond the minimum requisite health coverage, vacation, and sick days. The biggest hurdle for our applicants was that they needed to live in the area. A commute from other towns would simply not be economically viable on these part-time salaries.

Once we posted the two jobs, local people began to show up in our office. Darla was one of them. A massage therapist, Darla had invited me to join the women's gym soon after I moved to Pescadero. I had begun scheduling massages with her when I found myself getting too tense. And we had had numerous casual conversations in the post office parking lot over the years, discussing everything from religion and spirituality to whole-person health to Puente's ministry.

When Darla appeared in our office, she recounted her longstanding desire to work with our ministry. She told us she had worked for another nonprofit, raising money and writing grants. And she said she would be happy to be the first point of contact at the office to greet the men, take calls, receive donations and keep thank-you records on the computer. It was a natural fit. And so Darla became our new fund developer/office manager—and I had to find a new masseuse!

Having a staff required that we begin drafting our first "policies and procedures" notebook. Julia offered to share the text of the personnel manual she had created for the local dental clinic *Sonrisas* (Smiles), and Margaret contributed sample policies gleaned from the Internet. When a draft was completed, the board reviewed and adopted it. This assured fair and clear treatment for all staff and new hires as our organization began to grow.

As we prepared to open our doors, I ordered a beautiful new sign. In keeping with our desire to unite peoples and nations, I based the design of our new sign on the logo we'd created for our letterhead. We produced the arched bridge in five brilliant stripes—*verde, blanco, rojo, blanco* and *azul* (green, white, red, white, and blue), taken from the flags of both Mexico (green, white and red) and the United States (red, white and blue); the shared red stripe in the middle symbolized the shared life blood of both nations and the connection between the two countries. Connecting over the bridge were men, women, old folks, children, even a friend depicted in a wheelchair, and a dog![17] The only objection to that sign I ever heard was from an old friend who joked, "And where's the cat?" This new sign was paid for with a donation from a kind board member.

The wood used for the sign had a special history, too. It had come from the old outhouse door at our "flood house." Bill, a wonderful artist engaged to a woman in my exercise group, painstakingly painted our logo onto that old, weathered wood. The effect was dazzling! Bill and our landlord's father-in-law installed the new sign on the roof over our office. Taking into account the blustery weather that so often barreled in from the sea a mile to the west, they had to secure it with great ingenuity.

---

[17] This can be seen in full color on our website at www.no-longer-strangers.org.

I resisted a powerful urge to have a mural painted on the west end of the building, one that would greet incoming traffic from the ocean. There already was one powerful mural that had been designed and painted by a group of local youth as part of a summer program. I had heard about minor *chispas* (disagreements) when the design of that mural was in process. And while the successful handling of community feelings around that project had impressed us, we figured: why push the *fronteras* (boundaries) as the agency *recién llegada* (recently arrived), unknown, and working with The Men Alone?

The youth's mural was monumental and inspiring. It was two stories high on the outside wall of the high school gym in plain view of all who passed by. These young artists had depicted a wonderful blend of cultural images. The director of that summer project, also named Margaret, photographed the finished mural and entered it in a state contest. The picture of the mural was so stunning that it received first place in a competition with other California art projects created as part of a drug and alcohol prevention program. The picture was then sent to Washington and displayed in the halls of Congress. The young artists were flown to Washington where they toured the exhibit with California's Senator Barbara Boxer. Despite the fact that when the first sketches appeared there had been grumbles, in the end these young people received their accolades, and the mural became the pride of the town.

A few weeks after we moved into our new office, Carol and her husband donated a durable and comfortable bench for its front garden. I tutored some of the local townspeople in Spanish on that wonderfully accessible bench. Some of the moms sat on the bench while waiting for their kids to be dropped off by the school bus. And bicycle-riding tourists often stopped by that bench just to sit and rest. Puente Center was to become a multi-use community-welcoming site for all.

Wendy, *mi tocaya* (my namesake), and her dear friend George volunteered to plant a garden near that bench in the front parking area. Within a few days, three half-barrels and two low planter boxes appeared full of zingy, blue alyssum; pure white snow-on-the-mountain; deep burgundy and cheery yellow snap dragons; and fragrant, dainty, lacey pinks. Then two ten-gallon clay pots showed up filled with gleaming yellow daisy bushes! A gift from a local nurseryman.

Tocaya tended these beautiful flowers whenever she came to meetings or to drop off welcome bags. Between her visits, our men nursed the flowers and made sure they were watered. And sometimes I surprised everyone by gardening, too. It was a lifetime joy and passion of mine that few knew about. Jill, our landlady, graciously let us use her spigot *de cachete* (without cost). Now the outside of our center was *bien vivo* (brightly colored), eye-catching, and inviting.

We had planned all along to use *el salón* (the main room) of our Center as the new home for *La Sala*. In this spacious room, we hung pictures—the first of which was *La Virgen de Guadalupe* (The Virgin of Guadalupe). This was the gift I had received from the men who had been displaced from their camp. Other pictures—of workers, *Indios* (Mexican families), and bicycles—adorned the walls, along with *tela y tapetes* (handwoven cloth) and both the Mexican and U.S. flags. The men's favorite CDs were arranged next to the boom box, games were stacked around the room, and snacks overflowed from blue plastic bins. Comfortable chairs and three round tables covered with bright *manteles* (tablecloths) were assembled, ready for the men.

As soon as everything was in place, *La Sala*'s activities moved to the Center. Over the next months, our brothers would settle into this new space, gathering around the tables to play games, to chat, to enjoy a snack, or simply to rest (warm and dry). The room was soon filled with laughter, and the windows steamed up, as more bodies crowded in. Of course, in warm weather *La Sala* expanded out into the patio and parking lot in front of the building. Finally, we were in our very own place. Puente had *un hogar* (a home!)

Board members brought in new things every day. John, a friend from a United Church of Christ congregation in Ladera who lived out on the Coast, determined that he could build a tabletop shelf the width of our *salón* with space for several rolling storage bins underneath. He snagged one of our unemployed young men, and in a week the project was done. A gal for whom I had served as translator during a labor misunderstanding at Costanoa Resort, asked if we wished to have café curtains. ¡*Cómo no* (of course)! Within a couple of days she brought them in, and to our delight they were deep green to match our chairs. On the following afternoon, her beau installed the necessary hardware to hang them in the concrete block window frames. In the end, we had to purchase only one shelf for $3.75 at the local *pulguita* (the thrift shop).

But of course, we had to set up the office space, too. Margaret gathered all of Puente's paper files, copied all computer files onto CDs, and transferred everything to the new office. Chuck and several board members arranged for a new computer system after spending hours trying to jerry-rig my home computer to connect with my Palm. Another board member purchased chairs, yet another donated shelves and rugs, and still another brought us additional computers and set up phones. We received an office desk from a Latino community artist and ergonomically designed desk chairs from one of our trusted food program volunteer—everything we needed to set up a working center of operations alongside our drop-in site.

The first week of January 2005 we opened our doors with Darla as our new office manager. But we still needed to fill the Community Outreach Worker position, and so we revisited all the applications. One of our top candidates decided against the job after a visit to *La Sala*. It became obvious to her—and to us—that the job was located too far from her home. With soaring gas prices, and her children's transportation schedule, this was not the right match—despite the fact that she was both bilingual and bicultural!

Among the applicants for our COW position was a local high school senior, the son of Mexican immigrants. George had been born in this country and had grown up in the caretaker quarters of a local "Y" summer camp. He came to interview looking very professional in his starched, pink dress shirt, purple tie, dark sports coat, and slacks. His experience in peer counseling, his participation in Youth United Nations, and his other volunteer work around the community impressed us as solid preparation for our job. And he was known around town as "Guido's son," another favorable trait. He would make a great local role model for other community youth.

George had a number of school commitments that made it difficult for him to take on our half-time position during the school year. For one thing, he was on the baseball team. In a small high school like Pescadero's, everyone who was physically able played on a team. Otherwise, with such small numbers, the sports would have to be discontinued! (But what was a handicap in sports was an advantage in the classroom: this small school had great teacher-student ratios.) George also had a senior trip to Hawaii and prom night to schedule around. But even with these responsibilities, he found time to come in for a few hours each day until school was out.

George was a great team player, literally and figuratively—and hiring him took us one step further toward our goal of having a staff that reflected the cultural mix of the community. As a Mexican-American growing up in the United States, George was an example of a young man who did not lose his family's cultural values. Often he had to swap cars with a family member in order to pick up a sibling, and sometimes a younger brother or sister would sit around at *La Sala* waiting for him to finish work. George's family was, in turn, very proud that he now worked at a professional job in town. By the time school ended, we knew George pretty well. Board Members, staff and several volunteers attended his graduation, whooping and hollering with his family and friends. Directly after graduation, George began serving at Puente Center half time.

Despite his heritage, George did not know people who worked in the fields around town, had not heard the stories of border crossings, and was unfamiliar with current conditions in Mexico. It was difficult for him to understand the motivation of the men who had come north to work in our fields. "Why don't they just learn to speak English?" he once asked. "And why would they go through all that and leave their families

194

behind?"— not uncommon questions from many who worked with The Men Alone.

As George worked with the men, he began listening to their stories of border crossings, work hassles, family separation and loneliness. And he quickly gained a new appreciation for all that his own parents had gone through—the trials and tribulations they had endured so that he and his brother and sister could grow up in the United States. It was a great life lesson.

George made a strong contribution to our new organization. He tended to the personal issues of the men (a part of my ministry that was extremely hard for me to let go of). He maintained the food program and shuffled supplies from the elementary school's *almacén* (store room) to *La Sala*. And he input data into our new Access client database, which allowed us to accumulate the kinds of statistics that funders liked to see. He flew through that database like *una araña* (a spider)—an image that springs to mind from an experience I had when I worked in Puerto Rico. There I had met *la anciana* (the old woman) who wove *encaje* (lace), as deftly as any spider, with tiny "wooden spindles" and thread. She was called *la araña* (the spider) around her *aldea* (village) in the hills. It was such a joy to see George add his tools to our team, and especially his facility with technology, to our work!

Of course, I, too, moved my office to the new site. While a new computer, comfortable desk chair, and grand new phone system were all very exciting and welcoming, some days I actually found myself missing my familiar "office" at home. From home as I worked, I could enjoy year round views of the fields in their seasons and the workers at Levelea Farm. I had watched them plowing and planting and harvesting. Shouting a greeting from the porch to any passersby on bike or foot was my life's blood. I had to remind myself that in my new position, there were more and more grants to write, presentations to make, donations to be picked up, contacts to be made, resources to be investigated—all taking me away from the part that *me llenó más que todo~del alma y del espíritu* (buoyed my spirit and warmed my soul most): just *being* with our guys.

On May 5, 2005, the seventh anniversary of Puente Ministry and the fifth anniversary of *La Sala*, we invited everyone who had ever shown any interest in Puente to come to our Grand Opening Celebration. It was *Cinco de Mayo*,[18] and we gathered in the Puente parking lot, with The Men Alone standing ready to serve to the community a meal of rice, beans, and tamales, plus the *La Sala* favorite: tortilla chips and salsa.

This hospitable meal came from a gargantuan donation of food from *Los Amigos taquería*—except for the tamales, which were handmade by our own Guadalupe—Pescadero's resident "tamale mom." Every Thursday for years, her white van cruised through town to the pre-school parking lot she was bringing *sus tamaleras* (her big steamer pots) filled with tamales *vender* (to sell). The tamales were made *vegetariano, con pollo, con chile verde o rellenos* (vegetarian, with chicken, with spicy pork or stuffed with cheese)—wonderful delicacies that we clearly did not have the touch to make in our own kitchens. Often we purchased loaded paper plates of these tamales *para llevar* (to take home) and freeze for the following week's meals.

Some time after Ellen and I had moved to Pescadero, Guadalupe's family had the good luck to win—in a *rifa* (raffle)—the chance to live in a low-rent home in the Moon Ridge Village of Half Moon Bay twenty miles to the north of Pescadero. We thought nothing of driving to her new home to pick up her special dishes for a celebration or party. We did just that for our Grand Opening Celebration.

The tables overflowed with food, and *un bienvenido* (a warm welcome) was offered to all who showed up. Some of our guests came from as far away as Berkeley and Oakland. Others were locals just passing by—including bus drivers, business

---

[18] See en.wikipedia.org/wiki/Cinco de Mayo for details of the celebration in remembrance of a battle fought in Puebla against the French when the Mexicans unexpectedly prevailed. This is not Mexican Independence Day, which is celebrated annually on September 16 (en.wikipedia.org/wiki/Mexican War of Independence).

owners, our school district superintendent, and even curious onlookers. All were welcomed and fed!

We hung our Mexican and United States flags high above Puente Center's front door and just below our new sign. Inside, a video created by the San Francisco Foundation's Community Award committee,[19] and another produced by ABC Channel 7, told the story of Puente. At last we had a place to bask in the sunlight, to reflect that light upon each other, and to see more clearly the image of who we were becoming as a community. We took it all in, ate until we were filled, and shared our new place with one another. Nothing could have been sweeter.

The first video had been created by the San Francisco Foundation as a result of a Community Leadership Award we'd won after being nominated by Karen, then director of North Street Family Services. The San Francisco Foundation had arranged for this on-site video to explain who we were and whom we served. It came along with a $20,000 award. And best of all, we were told that the video would be screened at the Herbst Theater in San Francisco during a special awards ceremony to which we were, of course, all invited.

It was a dream come true—and on the Big Screen! We chose a group of The Men Alone to accompany us to the awards ceremony, and with Pancho, our bus driver, we drove up the Coast Highway to San Francisco. The men were astounded by the view and the lights of the city, and thrilled with the idea of being honored for what we—and they—considered to be ordinary hospitality. At a beautiful reception under the light of a full moon, we received our award. The brothers beamed with joyful pride in the life we had built together. And all of this had come from our understanding of Jesus' call and teaching.

Not long thereafter, ABC Channel 7's segment "People Who Make a Difference" honored my work at Puente by

---

[19] When Puente de la Costa Sur received the San Francisco Foundation Community Leadership Award in 2004, the Foundation commissioned Citizen Film to create this video. It can be viewed at www.no-longer-strangers.org/

producing and airing a several-minute film about our bike ministry.

And about that same time, I was awarded a Pacific School of Religion alumni award for my work founding Puente. During that awards ceremony, my mentor, the Rev. Dan Aprá, was also honored, in part for his years of support with Hispanic ministries. It was a wonderful day! Together Reverend Dan and I thanked all who inspired us, and served with us, and who found their blessings in sharing the grace of God and extravagant love wherever we worked and lived.

14

Celebrating a Future and a Hope

We are all citizens of one world...
Let us have but one end in view,
the welfare of humanity;
and let us put aside all selfishness
in consideration of language,
nationality, or religion

— John Comenius (1592-1670)

Barry Bonds, San Francisco Giants player, set up a special fund with Peninsula Community Foundation to offer front row bleacher seats, just above his position in the left field, to those who might not be able to afford to come to a game. The invitation to take some men to a ballgame came to Puente almost like comic relief. It arrived during the days when we were busy preparing our application for nonprofit status, hiring a real staff, and moving into our very own center—and I was learning to become an executive director. But "Take me out to the ball game!" We dropped everything!

We took ten men, some who had never seen a baseball game. They knew it was not their game of *fútbol* (soccer), but for a night at the ballpark, they didn't care what the game would be. They would be *saliendo* (going out)!

I warned the men that nights in San Francisco could be quite cold, but that first year they came in clean, short-sleeved shirts with only their smiling faces and *gorros* (caps) to keep them warm. On the ride to the park we held a *rifa* (raffle) for the one San Francisco Giants baseball cap we had been given, and the guy who won it proudly stepped off the bus that day sporting his official cap. As we walked past the lagoon to the stadium, the men had only two questions in their minds: would there be *muchachas* (girls)? And would *La Migra* (Immigration and Naturalization Services (INS), now called Immigration and Customs Enforcement (ICE)) pick them up?

We did see many beautiful women and girls at the game, and that fact warmed their hearts far more than watching Barry Bonds hit a homerun! For their viewing pleasure, we took the long way to our seats—up the stairs, around the "homerun lagoon," across the bleacher section, under the Coca-Cola bottle slide, and past the huge baseball mitt.

That night we insisted that the men stay in groups chaperoned by a volunteer, even when going to the restroom or to buy food. No one knew how dangerous this sortie could be for a man "attending while brown." But, of course, sometime between the fourth and ninth inning, Tino slipped away. Happily, he rejoined the group with no negative consequences. It was quite a challenge to keep these mature men in tow!

Not surprisingly, it was cold that evening, and so we stoked up with hot dogs, burgers, fries, sodas and hot chocolate. The following year, when we were again offered tickets, the men remembered that first brisk evening and actually showed up in their warmest *chaquetas* (jackets)!

Baseball wasn't our only special outing. A board member offered us a dozen *boletos* (tickets) to attend a local rodeo in San Gregorio. She had scouted out the schedule and seating during the previous weekend to be sure that the occasion would please the men. Of course, we accepted the offer.

Hizo mucho calor (It was sweltering hot) that Sunday, a better day for the beach than a rodeo, but the men were in their element. They knew about rodeos. Their hometowns had them. And so that day they taught us more than we ever thought there was to know about horses, roping, calves and clowns! ¡*Qué bonito fue* (How beautiful it was) to see them laughing and reminiscing together! A few of them wore their snazzy snakeskin boots and cowboy shirts, dressed like they would have dressed at home for such an event.

We invited one of our associate conference ministers, Rev. Edgar, to join us that day. A Filipino by heritage, he was able to understand at least some Spanish. He'd never been to a rodeo and was unfamiliar with much that our brothers took for granted. He took it all in, asking numerous questions in his broken Spanish to get to the salient points. He was *encantado* (delighted) by it all—the gargantuan beef sandwiches with onion and green peppers; the powerful animals; and the cowboys, youth and children all displaying their riding and roping skills.

The gift of that outing was so appropriate for The Men Alone, a real connection with their life back home and one they could not have imagined attending with their limited resources. It became obvious to me that day that we had become one community, supporting one another through the sad, hard times—and now enjoying each other in the fun times, too.

I remember this period as being rich and rewarding, full of new people and unexpected events, and I truly loved being in the midst of all that was happening. But at the same time, I felt very isolated, and I looked forward each week to phone chats with my professional coach, Beryl. Having that outside voice of experience to listen to my concerns, to ask provocative questions, and to give wise counsel was essential to my well-being during that time.

My regular visits with my spiritual director, Paula, were quite different, yet equally important. I carried to her all my ponderings, listening for her spiritual comments—and together we searched for the hand of God in all that was happening. She offered a perspective that no one living or working with me could provide, and I remain grateful for it to this day. It became clear to me that anyone in a role such as mine needed to have these kinds of people supporting them from the outside.

And yet, as the months came and went, I could not deny that this period of my life was drawing to a close. I was beginning to think about retirement. Fortunately, Pat, a longtime colleague who was executive director of her own organization, told me that she too was preparing to retire. She and I agreed to meet for lunch once a month while we walked this path together. We talked about how we hoped to let go of our relationships with our agencies, leaving them with someone who might share our visions. Together we affirmed the mysterious presence of God in our day-to-day work and the changes coming to both of us.

And then, all too soon, it was time for me to go. I knew that when I left I would need to stay away from my community in Pescadero for at least a year. This is the practice for pastors when they leave a parish: it allows for a clean transition to new leadership.

Our consultant had mentioned "succession planning" when we first began our preparations to become a nonprofit, so I knew it was coming. As I talked with other agency founders and executive directors, it became clear that if a founder truly wanted the work of the organization to continue, she or he needed to be willing to retire while the organizational energies were high, while the board was full of enthusiasm, and while funding sources were strong. Clearly now was time for me to set in motion my own plans for retirement at age sixty-two, and to be ready to listen to God's voice for the rest of my life.

And so I began looking for a place to start my new life. Ellen and I talked over the idea of moving out of our little house in Pescadero and renting a place on the other side of the hills, closer to her work. For the past seven years, she had been making a daily commute of nearly thirty miles each way. While the trip took her through beautiful territory—the road was bordered by glorious fields of flowers and picturesque ocean beaches, sometimes even haloed by firey oranges, reds, purples and pinks in a dazzling sunrise or sunset, or the ghostly white reflections of moonrise or moonset—it was still a long commute, and it ate up many hours of her day. Maybe now was the time to change that.

In the end, we did give up the little house in Pescadero. We rented an even smaller apartment in San Mateo just a couple of blocks from her office. This gave her a five-minute commute, literally a walk through the park!

My transitional plan was to spend my final year before retirement working in Pescadero four short days each week. I wanted George to bond with the men on his own, and Darla to have the freedom to build Puente's list of local contacts in her own way. We arranged my work so that I could do much of it from home, and so that when I did make the drive, I would do it during non-rush-hour times. I began to ease into the separation process, mentoring others to carry on the spirit of our service and to nurture our precious relationships.

As I unpacked the last box in San Mateo, I admitted to Margaret that I already missed living among the fields, walking to the post office, and seeing everyone. It was not the same conducting my work via phone, email and occasional meetings. I missed the brothers—and all of our friends on the Coast. Nonetheless, I knew it was the right decision, an important step to be taking.

At about that time, the Peninsula Community Foundation urged another passage. Dick suggested that leaders of the three organizations serving families, children, and single men in Pescadero consider combining their services into one agency. Not only could space be shared, but now there would be an opportunity to become one body, an evolution that would foster sustainability for us all. We three nonprofits could not continue to draw on the area's limited resources—foundation grants, willing volunteers, and able board members—over the long term. To have a single site, board, and administration could be beneficial to us all. And recruiting to fill staff positions would be much easier with one agency.

In confidential meetings from April through September, I worked with Eileen, the interim director from North Street, to discern the best way to continue providing services to our community and to fulfill our mission with the men. It was a really difficult time. I was not able to maintain a light heart, and I often felt sick to my stomach as I considered letting go of Puente's singular attention to The Men Alone. What if they got lost in the shuffle? What if they were left once again on the street—or in the shadows of their own souls?

What an opportunity for growth and trust for me! It was time for me to move on, and to let God accompany our brothers. Working through our staff, God would widen our bridge from one lane, limited to one group, to one that offered access for everyone. Our expanded bridge would engender self-esteem and self-motivation in everyone within our community, whether they were recently arrived or had generations of history in our village. I needed to heed this new calling and to let go. As Dick, my program officer, reminded me: "You must do this for the men, Wendy." And he was right.

Ultimately, the family services of North Street Community Resource Center joined with Puente Ministry to become the Puente Resource Center, ready to go when the new interim director appeared in December. It was both a grief and relief to my heart. The men would be well cared for and Puente would carry on. And the " mom-and-pop start-up" ministry that had been my heart's work would become the foundation and cornerstone of a new, combined agency. We are now but a part of the bigger calling, thanks be to God.

In my last fall as executive director, we enjoyed a deeply moving "*El Día de los Muertos*" (Day of the Dead) festival at the home of our board member Nancy. The men came late, no surprise to me: they had been at *el cementario* (the cemetery) honoring the short life of a dear thirteen-year-old whom one of our brothers called *familia* (family). Once they arrived, they began sharing their stories of border crossings, and of the pain they felt in leaving family behind. That pain was sometimes fresh even after a decade or more: one of our brothers told of being here twenty years without going home. They also spoke of the number of funerals they had missed since they came north. And they shared other memories that go with this special time—memories of *ofrendas* (altars) with precious photos of the dead; *cempasúchil anaranjados bien vivos* (bright, orange marigolds) so commonly associated with this day; and traditional *refrescos* (refreshments)—*mole* (spicy chocolate sauce), *tamales y sopapillas* (fried pastry) and *galletas con calaveras* (cookies decorated with skull shapes).

All too soon, it was Thanksgiving—and the Belmont church and community volunteers served turkey and tamales in true "family style." Our gathered "family of choice" included folks from over the hill, up the Coast, and out at the ranches and nurseries—and still we would have made room for more from the highways and byways.

The first Sunday of Advent, that next weekend, was my birthday, and I preached my final sermon at the Pescadero church. I said my tearful goodbyes to those gathered that morning. It was a tender and heartfelt leave-taking because I knew I would not return to the parish for at least a year. For Ellen and me, Pescadero Community Church would no longer be "our" place to worship. I needed to be grateful, to say my *despedidas* (goodbyes), and to let the community go.

My last major celebration with the people I loved here came on December 8 during the festival of *La Virgen de Guadalupe* (The Virgin of Guadalupe). Two volunteers—A. J. from Belmont, and Wendy, *mi tocaya* (my namesake), from Pescadero—collaborated to take a group to San Juan Bautista, two hours south, to participate in the festival as it is performed in the old mission chapel there. It would be an event celebrated in drama, song and dance. After several individuals donated funds to cover transportation and meals for the men, we gathered nearly sixty folks—including workers, board members, community neighbors, relatives, spouses, and staff. We loaded everyone into a SamCoast bus and a fleet of borrowed cars. Being green-conscious, we chose for the trek only those cars that were hybrids or that had high gas mileage.

The Men Alone were *bien vestido* (all dressed up)—the likes of which we had not seen except during the few *bailes* (dances), *bautizos* (baptisms) and *quinceañeras* (15-year-olds' coming-out parties) that had taken place over the years. We formed *un desfile* (a caravan) and drove those beautiful back roads through the golden foothills to our destination. It was a long trip, but at long last we reached the town of San Juan Bautista—and the tasty buffet that awaited us. It was worth the wait! We ordered pitchers of soda, and the men ate their fill. Then we wandered the streets of this artsy tourist community and purchase a few mementos. We sold off a few extra tickets, took some photos of one another, and gathered to wait in line for seats in the pews of the old church.

The presentation brought tears to all of us. People of all ages participated, using the Nahuatl language along with historically accurate music and instruments. It was an immersion in the spirit of the season far beyond the Hallmark Christmas that most people come to expect. Many of the men remarked that they had never seen such a pageant so beautifully choreographed and gloriously represented through native dress, language, music, and staging. Others simply mulled over pleasant memories of similar celebrations at home. What a gorgeous day—in a chapel beside an historic cemetery, with a statue of San Juan Bautista overlooking the fertile valley. We were fed in spirit and body as we shared our reverence for the Virgin with the gathered family of God.

On the way back, our faithful community bus driver Pancho showed his sensitivity by letting the men stop for a late night snack and to purchase some *comestibles* (groceries). Good thing we did all this on a Sunday, their only day off! That day, from morning to late night, we celebrated being a community by sharing an adventure—*una jira* (a fieldtrip)—like none other in Puente history. And at the center of it all were our brothers.

But there was one more event that would cap off my time in Pescadero. Staff had sequestered themselves for weeks with various board members and volunteers, quietly plotting and planning a wonderful farewell celebration on my behalf. It was supposed to be a complete surprise for me. And it was!

Invitations—little works of art created with *bien vivos* (bright, lively) colors on special paper—were mailed to all of Puente's faithful volunteers, staffers and supporters over the years. They were also posted where the men lived in Pescadero. Food was ordered from Guadalupe, from Los Amigos taquería, and from Cindy's Market—and for the very first time, Cindy prepared the thick, rich, chocolate-spicy sauce known as mole. Groups of friends decorated the original *La Sala* site in the Native Sons' Hall with vegetables and fruit, cornucopias overflowing. This special room had been tastefully restored— walls painted, woodwork stained, windows redone, a beehive removed, mice and rats shut out, bathrooms and kitchen remodeled. These friends knew that this was to be our last sacrament—a meal to be shared with our family of choice. All was ready for the people of God.

Over a hundred people gathered there on that bright December afternoon. There were representatives from the San Mateo County Board of Supervisors; the UCC conference office; the Belmont, Pescadero, Pleasant Hill and Berkeley churches; and more. Our media friends came, as did grant officers, technical assistants, counselors, and both local and county agency heads. My mentor, the Rev. Dan Aprá, and his wife, Joy, showed up, as did many of the people who had supported Puente right from the start—Ellen, Margaret and Peter, the staff and the board. Everyone ooh-ed and aah-ed over the lovely table decorations: heavy linen-like envelopes with historic picture postcards of Pescadero for each person. The tables filled quickly, especially the ones up front reserved for The Men Alone, our brothers.

The men were celebrated that day, too. They were not asked to set up or clean up as they did on normal *La Sala* days; they simply shared "their house" with dozens of friends and soon-to-be friends. "¡Mi casa es su casa (may my house be your house)!" Smiling, they took their seats at the reserved tables, with the confidence that they belonged there. How different from my first encounters years before! Today they would not slide by in the shadows or stay in the fields or barracks. They would not lean against a wall waiting for a job. Now they were spotlighted as full members of the community. Together we had built a bridge, sharing laughter and joy, grief and sadness, all of life's gifts, in community.

That afternoon was filled with speakers, skits, and songs. Everyone who wished to be was photographed, and all were invited to add comments to my memory book. I received a very generous parting *regalo* (gift)—a coupon to buy a kayak that would allow me to set out on many a peaceful paddle throughout the rest of my life! All this took place on a Sunday afternoon, during traditional *La Sala* time—and what a "community living room" we had that day! *¡Qué lindo* (how gorgeous)!

Finally, it was time to say *vaya con Dios* (God be with you). The hard reality—that I would remove myself from this village—began to set in. We had lived and worked together for nearly ten years, a decade of changes, and now it was time to turn to the next call. What I had planted and nurtured was ready to bolt—to shoot up, to flower, and to create seeds for the next growth spurt.

A comfort in all this leave-taking came when I heard that the board had appointed Kerry Lobel—a long-time volunteer, friend, neighbor, and colleague—as Puente's interim executive director. Kerry had significant experience in directing national, justice-seeking, advocacy, and spiritually-based nonprofit organizations. And though I was perfectly aware of her experience and abilities, it had never occurred to me to invite her to apply to be Puente's executive director. I had thought that, with all her past experience, the position at Puente would seem too limited an opportunity. Kerry's appointment became yet another grace in my process of leaving things decently and in order (I Corinthians 14:40), in keeping with my Presbyterian roots. I knew that the well-being of The Men Alone would be in good hands.

A few days later as I sat with Margaret paging through my Memory Book, she began reminiscing about that special day.

"The moment I will never forget," she said quietly, "was just before we sat down to eat, when most of the guests were standing by their seats. The door opened, and the last busload of guys filed in, grinning and all cleaned up, and took their places at the big round table right up front next to the buffet. At that moment all the rest of the guests simply surrounded the men. Who would have thought that all this would come from you talking to a few of the workers passing by the church and deciding to hand out reflectors!"

Who would have thought, indeed! It was a simple practice of radical hospitality that had produced Puente. And for as long as men cross that dangerous border between Mexico and the United States to work in the fields of Pescadero, they will be able to find a bridge of compassion in our town. They will find a warm welcome, basic survival supplies, and a home away from home here on the other side. During one special time, in one special place, we found a way to truly live out our United Church of Christ motto: *That they may all be one.*

Acknowledgments

I give thanks for the many who have brought me safe, taught me, and mentored me thus far: my wife and partner, Ellen Sweetin; my parents, Marge and Bill Taylor; my sister, Cathy Witham; my mentor and friend Margaret Cross; the late Rev. Dan Aprá; the Congregational Church of Belmont, United Church of Christ; the Rev. John Brooke and the Reverend Karen Gale; Barbara Turner and Janet Murphy, along with both of our Pescadero interns, Billie Soriano and the Reverend Monique Ortiz; my retirement "crone" Pat Brown; and the teachers at Mark Morris High School, Whitworth College, the University of Washington, and Pacific School of Religion, all of whom showed me the depth of a liberal arts education and led me in a wide spiral of spiritual growth, through pastoral and theological studies, language training, and even the practicalities of administration. For all these precious personal and spiritual relationships, I am grateful.

It is a continuing surprise to me that I ended up founding a nonprofit agency way beyond my ecclesiastical skills. ¡Sí se puede (yes, anyone can)! My inspiration was drawn from my years at the Longview Community Church, United Fellowship of Metropolitan Churches, Ladera Community Church and Hayward Eden United Church of Christ. During those years, I was also guided by Sister Mary Ann Scofield of the Spiritual Directors Institute at the Mercy Center in California; by my spiritual directors the Reverend Nancy McKay and Paula Baldwin; and by my coaches Kerry Lobel, Nancy Raulston and Beryl Rullman. Through my ordination process, I was especially inspired by our denomination, with whom we are no longer strangers: the United Church of Christ—an Open and Affirming Church, and a Just Peace Church, in the flesh. Later I could even be heartened by those churches who during my candidating were not yet ready to be Open and Affirming in my call and ordination process.

I realize now that, in times flung far and wide, I was also inspired by *César Chávez*; Volunteers in Service to America (VISTA) Corps; Wycliffe Bible Translators in Perú; Witness for Peace in Nicaragua; the Reverend Dr. Robert MacAfee Brown; the Archbishop Oscar Romero; Henri J. M. Nouwen; Gustavo Gutiérrez, O.P.; and the Western Hispanic Ministries Strategy Team of the United Church of Christ. Finally, I offer my gratitude to the late Reverend Orril Fluharty, and to the rural Pescadero Community Church, United Church of Christ, which delighted in having me accompany their new mission with an entire community of Spanish- and English-speaking saints.

For all of you who supported our ministry with financial, hands-on, and spiritual sustenance—including our Board of Directors; local faith communities; clergy colleagues; sister agencies; Bay Area foundations staff; consultants (especially Regina Neu); San Mateo County health department; print and television media in San Mateo, San Jose, San Francisco; and local neighbors, family, friends and volunteers— it could not have happened without all of you. And finally, my deep gratitude to our process readers, those half-dozen friends including—Peter (Margaret's husband) and my Ellen—who asked all the right questions and shared their hope. A very special thanks to our editing and publishing consultant, Holly Brady, who came to us serendipitously and by the grace of God, and without whose urging and fresh perspectives we might never have seen this miracle—our "story"—on paper.

Mil gracias y les aprecio profundamente.
Thank you, I appreciate you all so deeply.

¡Qué Dios les bendiga!
May God bless you all!

¡Qué les vayan bien!
May your lives go well!

— *Wendy Taylor*

Appendices

Caminante, no hay puentes,
se hace puentes al andar.

Voyager, there are no bridges.
One builds them as one walks.

— Gloria E. Anzaldúa,
This Bridge Called My Back, pg. v

Appendix 1:
Building a Compassionate Community

Are you drawn to the idea of a compassionate community? Here's a possible roadmap on how to proceed:

Step 1: Explore Your Own Surroundings First

- **Stay put!** If you feel moved to reach out beyond your usual circle, stop and look around. There are areas in your own neighborhood, city, county, and state that may be at least as foreign to you as other countries. Explore your local schools, streets, apartment buildings, and businesses for areas of opportunity. Then share what you find with your friends.

- **Read, view films, listen to music, dance, taste authentic foods, join in celebrations** of other cultural groups in your area. Again, share what you discover with your friends and family.

- **Absorb all you can from the young people** in your life who are probably already at home in a mix of cultures, languages, and classes. They often are, without much anguish, reveling in the rich diversity around them. Humbly ask them to teach you, take you, show you, explain to you, introduce you to their friends who are no longer strangers. (Be teachable, of course.)

- **Start small.** Find little ways to educate others within your circle of friends. Don't get paralyzed, thinking it's all too big.

Step 2: Leave Your Comfort Zone

- **Volunteer (while still in your own locale).** See what a difference you can make right near home. If you find you enjoy it, watch out!

- **Don't try to do it all yourself**—especially if you notice that others are not participating. That's a real model for speedy burnout.

- **Consider traveling to parts of Mexico** beyond the tourist/cruise cities. Educate yourself so that you understand personally how these workers and families live. You will quickly come to understand why they have come to the United States in pursuit of their dream of a better life.

Step 3: When You Feel Ready, Build Your Compassionate Community

- **Walk with the Community.** Go out and just chat. It is our belief that newcomers of every language, culture, race, orientation, or political view long to be welcomed and heard. We can, as faithful people, invite conversation without judgment and be open to all views. As we do, we will grow.

- **Find ways to engage others**, not just friends or ones who look like us, to find out how similar we are. Learn to talk to community leaders, agencies, government officials, and law enforcement officers early on. See the Christ in the eyes of every new person you encounter.

- **Organize the "regulars"—those unofficial leaders and stalwarts.** Start with the "choir" so that the core group— the role models—are known to others in the area. Insist that each group member be accorded the respect and care offered to "strangers." Build up this small core of local workers and bring them together regularly. Demonstrate to others that this group is safe, that the lion and lamb can dwell together safely.

- **Collaborate with existing organizations** that have similar goals or that already interact with the community you intend to serve. Sometimes you will find it most expedient to augment the systems already in place instead of "reinventing the wheel."

- **Taking small steps, build it.** They will come, including sponsors and advisors.

Step 4: Practice a New Way of Being With Others

- **Learn to hold one another as family,** assuming the best, and making allowances for balance everyday.

- **Remove from your mind the "entitlement of white privilege"** and simply work toward blending your culture with the culture of the group you are serving.

- **Ask one another what is important, joyous, difficult.** Pray for each other, and offer resources when you can. This will not be easy: we are often not able to be *that* intimate even with our familiars.

- **Remember that no one has the *right* way to minister with another**—no matter the culture.

- **Learn from each other,** and work toward agreement in small steps.

- **Reflect on the questions** posed in the training references and the biblical reflections found on our website: www.no-longer-strangers.org.

- **Continually check** with your peer group, a youth group in your community, or colleagues at your work place to assess your own cultural humility and willingness to advocate for access for all.

- **Act upon your beliefs,** draw on your experiences, and call on others to support progress toward integrity. You will feel better, as will the "strangers among you," who may even be your own in-laws, siblings or parents. A compassionate community embodies God's love for all, the blessings of Divine abundance, and our inherent interconnectedness. What could be better!

Remember:
Always extend an *extravagant welcome.*
This is the spiritual practice of *radical hospitality.*

Appendix 2:
Resources

Books

- **Lacy, Marilyn, RSM.** *This Flowing Toward Me: A Story of God Arriving as Stranger.* **Indiana: Ave Maria Press, 2009.**
  A Sister of Mercy details her experiences working with refugees around the world.

- **Miles, Sara.** *Take this Bread: A Radical Conversion.* **New York: Ballantine Books, 2007.**
  Sara Miles tells the story of establishing a food bank in a San Francisco church sanctuary to serve sisters and brothers in need.

- **Mosley, Don with Joyce Hollyday.** *Faith Beyond Borders: Doing Justice in a Dangerous World.* **Nashville: Abingdon Press, 2010.**
  A co-founder of Habitat for Humanity and Jubilee Partners focuses on how he built community among refugees. This model is perhaps most like Puente, except that it occurs within the context of housing and resettlement.

- **Muñoz Ryan, Pam.** *Esperanza Rising.* **New York: Scholastic Inc., 2000.**
  A young girl and her mother, forced to flee their Mexican ranch, find refuge in a farm workers' camp in California. For ages 8-12.

- **Roque Hernández, Lamberto.** *Cartas a Crispina.* **Oaxaca: Carteles Editores, 2002.**
  Touching and poetic stories of dislocated immigrants from Oaxaca as told through letters. Each letter is in Spanish; a vulnerable and truthful conclusion in English covers the entire body of experiences.

- **Russell, Letty M.** *Just Hospitality: God's Welcome in a World of Difference.* **Louisville: Westminster John Knox Press, 2009.**
  Lectures delivered at Yale Divinity School.

Films/DVDs

- 2009 *The Other Side of Immigration* – documentary on the economic conditions underpinning the decisions of migrant workers.

- 2007 *Under the Same Moon* — The story of a Mexican mother who comes to the US to work, and her son who decides to make the harrowing journey to join her there.

- 2007 *Which Way Home* – documentary about children who, left behind by their parents, travel from Latin America through Mexico to the United States .

- 2006 *Babel* – subtitled, four-language/four country film with a powerful segment on the Mexican border crossing of a grandmother and her grandchild.

- 2004 *Puente de la Costa Sur* – short documentary commissioned by The San Francisco Foundation (www.sff.org) when Puente de la Costa Sur received The San Francisco Foundation Community Leadership Award. Created by Citizen Film (**www.citizenfilm.org**).

- 2004 *Mojados: Through the Night* – documentary following four workers in a border crossing.

- 1983 *El Norte* – Impoverished Guatemalan teens cross into the United States hoping for a better life.

Websites

- AlterNet
  www.alternet.org/immigration

- *No Longer Strangers* book website
  www.no-longer-strangers.org

- Puente de la Costa Sur
  www.puentedelacostasur.org or **www.mypuente.org**

Language Learning

Practice your language skills in your community wherever possible. Visit day-laborer centers where workers go to find jobs in their communities. Go to the "mission" district in your city on a regular basis and become "the other." "Walk a mile" in the shoes of someone else. Travel out of your comfort zone.

For Mexico, Central America and South America in-home programs and language schools:
- **Casa Xelaju** in Quetzaltenango, Guatemala
  www.casaxelaju.com or 612-235-4347

For United States language learning opportunities:
- **Lake Tahoe Community College Intensive Spanish Summer Institute** – a multilevel, non-traditional, interactive program for the whole family. Travel abroad programs can be arranged to study Spanish in Mexico or Spain.
  http://www.ltcc.edu/programs.asp?scatID=55

- **Local adult school or community college classes**

- **Rosetta Stone CD-ROMs** for use at home
  www.rosettastone.com

223

- **English as a Second Language (ESL) classes** where you might tutor and get to know native Spanish speakers

Immersion Experiences

In Mexico
- **Guadalupe Retreat Center/Weston Priory** Cuernavaca education and meeting the contexts out of which workers and families have come.
  www.westonpriory.org

On the Border
- **BorderLinks**
  A bi-national organization birthed in the 1980s out of the Sanctuary Movement and located in Tucson, Arizona. Includes education about experiences in both Latin America and North America.
  www.borderlinks.org

- **Centro Romero in San Ysidro, California**
  An agency that offers immersion trips, classes, theological discussions, and opportunities for small groups to be present at the border.
  www.ucc.org/justice/centro-romero/files/the-daniel-f-romero-center-for-border-ministries-brochure.pdf

- **Humane Borders/Fronteras Compasivas**
  An Arizona-based agency that conducts border work, including cleaning the regions where migrants cross and making water available in the desert. Includes a retreat site run by Disciples of Christ and United Church of Christ volunteers and staff.
  www.humaneborders.org

Through Faith Communities

- **United Church of Christ and Disciples of Christ**
  www.ucc.org/news/ucc-disciples-engage-issues

- **No More Deaths/No Más Muertes**
  An agency, born in 2004 from a multi-faith border conference, that follows the belief: *Humanitarian aid is never a crime.* The organization is currently a ministry of the Tucson Unitarian Universalists church.
  www.NoMoreDeaths.org or **www.uuctucson.org**

- *Quaker Action,* **American Friends Service Committee Newsletter, Spring 2011, volume 02, number 1, "Focus on Immigration"**
  An excellent resource for learning about actions, volunteering, border issues, immigrant stories, cultural immersions and media recommendations.
  www.afsc.org

Book Website

- *No Longer Strangers: The Practice of Radical Hospitality*
  We include on our website a video and photo gallery, author bios and contact information, links to important resources, and more.
  www.no-longer-strangers.org

About the Authors

Rev. Wendy J. Taylor is a retired pastor
in the United Church of Christ
and a teacher from Longview, Washington.
She graduated from Whitworth College and
the Pacific School of Religion. She lives with her wife,
Ellen Sweetin, in the Pacific Northwest.

Margaret Kimball Cross is a writer and
an award-winning community activist
from Waterloo, Iowa. She graduated from
State University of Iowa and now resides
with her husband, Peter, in Northern California.

✍

Wendy Taylor welcomes the opportunity to share with
interested audiences the experiences—and the human face—of
immigrant farm workers in Northern California.

She also enjoys speaking on how to build and sustain
community faith-based nonprofit service organizations.

To inquire about a speaking engagement, contact us via
www.no-longer-strangers.org